HOLISTIC PSYCHOLOGY OF ALEXANDER PINT

Not Sleeping in the Dream

By ALEXANDER PINT

Translated by Emin Kuliev, MD

www.pint.ru

https://caterpillartobuterfly.wordpress.com

Visit www.SkyrocketPress.com

Cover art by Freydoon Rassouli
ISBN: 978-1-944722-05-0

My deepest gratitude to everyone who directly or indirectly took part in the process of creating this book.
-Alexander Pint

"I don't teach you how to live; I show you how you live." - Alexander Pint

TABLE OF CONTENTS

CHAPTER 1: FIND DUALITY, AND YOU WILL FIND THE EXIT.. 1

How interested are you in becoming aware of yourself?............1

To relax from life...3

Where does this impulse for self-awareness come from? 5

Personality expresses only one side of duality...........................8

This reality is not built on understanding.
It is built on agreement..9

Why don't I understand myself? 11

What can you say about yourself?...13

Not understanding others is a consequence of
not understanding oneself..14

The script of your dream...16

Death is the greatest illusion of this reality.............................18

The popular killer 20

Self-identification "Disabled"..22

How duality works 24

From disease to health and back...25

CHAPTER 2: WHO IS THE WINNER IN THE FIGHT WITH HIMSELF? 29

Who will win if your right hand triumphs over
your left hand? 29

The correct self-investigation 31

Get to know the theme of your life..32

When duality is ripe, you can open it 35

What does the dead one feel?..38

How the hysteria of war is created...39

Distrustful trust or the duality of "faith—lack of faith" 41

Profitable sides of poverty 44

"I am happy, but I am proud…"..47

We realize what we are afraid of...49

Every suffering is based on condemnation and guilt................51

On four bonds that exist between two people..............................54

From essence to the personage and back 55

Who is the witness in the marriage of the mind and the heart? .58

False information is fragmented information 61

There is nothing here but illusions 62

CHAPTER 3: DEPENDENT INDEPENDENCE 65

"As I was driving a bus, my wallet was
stolen from my purse."..65

The power of your character manifests itself in resistance 66

"I am not irritated by my irritation any more…"........................68

Experiencing the duality "harshness—softness"........................70

Love—Connection of inner separation 73

I have activated the duality "rich—poor"....................................74

To discuss your problem instead of asking someone
to solve it 76

When does a social animal find its life successful?....................79

A human being creates problems to receive experience.............80

Human language was created to describe technical devices, not the
life of a spirit 81

Humanity's standing at the doorstep of
understanding the mind...83

In listening to what I say but not understanding
what I transmit, you cannot catch the essence of the message ..85

Self-investigation is investigation of the essence of the experiences
we are currently in 86

You cannot define the soul. You can only experience it. 88

Your soul directs your show, but do you hear what it says? 91

Find dependency in independence 92

Where does the exit out of dependency lead? 95

The fight for independence is fought to change the rules 97

Every child depends on his parents.

That's what leads him to rebel. 99

Familial matrix of fears is transmitted to us by our parents..... 102

What don't we study self-investigation in middle school? 105

CHAPTER 4: THE ILLUSIONS—INHERITANCE THAT PARENTS

PASS ON TO THEIR CHILDREN **107**

Faith that is based on fear leads to the materialization of fear 107

We inherit our parents' fears 109

Look for duality everywhere and in everything! 111

"You acquire experience by talking to us, and you take

our money for it. I condemn you for that…". 113

"Start relating to you daughter the way you wanted your parents to

relate to you when you were a little girl…". 114

Any ideal is an inner district attorney who condemns you to play

the role of a slave. 116

Ideal—an illusory answer to the main question. 118

East and West. How do their ideals interact? 121

Esoteric consumer society 122

Materialism and idealism—two sides of one coin 124

The average temperature in a hospital is normal 127

Money is a means. The main question is "What is it for?" 129

Criminal police or honest thief? 131

For most people, life means survival. 132

Two opposite directors of one show. 134

Deceit and honesty. 135

CHAPTER 1

FIND DUALITY, AND YOU WILL FIND THE EXIT

•❖•❖•❖•❖•❖•❖•❖•❖•❖•❖•❖•❖•

How interested are you in becoming aware of yourself?

— What interests our minds? Are our minds interested in awareness? The mind itself, the way it is now, is not interested in seeing how it works. It works mechanically, and it is not interested in revealing its mechanical nature. It is interested in satisfying the fluctuation of the dualities that are inculcated into it.

The mind works like a wave: it ascends on a "plus" — "very interesting", and then descends to a "minus" — "not interesting". The amplitude of these fluctuations may be high or low, but that is how our minds work; they will not work any other way. The intention to become whole or enlightened, which is the essence of our process, lies outside this amplitude; it just observes how the conditioned, dual mind works. We discuss everything our minds come up with during our seminars and webinars. We investigate and get to know how our minds deliver information—they use a certain sine wave. However, the mind itself cannot see how it operates. This work can be done only by exiting the borders of the conditioned mind. That is what we do here.

This work is not common here. Only a small number of people manifest interest in this work while most people are happy with the way their conditioned minds work.

I recently saw a movie produced by the BBC called *The Human Body*. It shows and discusses the stages through which a human body passes from birth to death. The movie portrays a human body as a well-functioning and well-regulated mechanism, which operates based on certain programs.

For example, sexual development occurs during adolescence. Many hormones are released according to a certain program. These hormones penetrate certain organs and change them. This happens irrespective of whether you want these changes to occur or not. Young boys and girls compare this process to a rollercoaster; they have no control over it. A kind of revolution occurs inside the body. The program that starts and controls the way these changes would proceed gets downloaded during the prenatal period. It gets activated many years later.

A human being has an apparatus—the physical body with which he goes through his life journey. The script of a life journey is downloaded into the mind as a set of imprints. Later, these imprints navigate and move the physical body by creating the situations some people call fate. How are these imprints downloaded? Why does your fate have certain specific nuances? How does it work in the case of an individual human being, and in civilization in general? Few people ask these questions, and those who do ask don't seem to find good answers. Those are the questions we ask here. We want to exit the borders of the conditioned mind, i.e. to enter another world.

A human being is a three-centered being: mind, body, and soul. We can see that our physical bodies are well-regulated mechanisms. Notwithstanding very difficult life scenarios inculcated into the mind, the body performs its role and usually functions quite well all the way to late adulthood. Currently, in most western countries, a physical body can function well for sixty or seventy years. Irrespective of the heavy pressures that the conditioned mind applies to the body, the body continues to work and perform its function.

The main direction of our process is to exit the borders of the conditioned mind. To come to know the mind is to know the fate of a human being and the laws that build it. The impulse necessary to conduct this work is currently quite rare in people. Where does this impulse come from, and why does it appear? I know that this impulse is very strong in me. I see that some people become attracted to it. I would call this impulse self-awareness.

To relax from life

— *It became clear to me that because of certain external reasons, I would not be able to attend this seminar. I recently got a new job. It is very demanding. I am also finishing college, and finals are coming up. On the other hand, I have been feeling very lonely lately. I found your books. I've read them, and I felt I need to be here. But the external circumstances … I felt I needed some rest … too much is happening at once. At the same time, I have not been to a better seminar than yours.*

— But at the same time, you create the conditions when you cannot come to the seminar. You create them yourself. Do you understand that?

— *Yes, I understand that.*

— We frequently hear people say, "I want to do that so badly, but I don't have the money, or I don't have the time, or I am sick and can't go." People usually reply, "Yes, of course, you can come next time." I am not going to say that. I will reinforce the situation for you to see your parts that create the situations that prevent you from coming here. I will say, "You have created this situation yourself." Become aware of your parts that believe that your habitual work and thoughts are more important than your being here. Until you see these parts, you will not be able to understand what is most important for you.

I don't know how your mind relates to what I say. Some of you may accuse me by saying, "He wants too much. I have things that are very important for me, for example, my finals." But I will insist that there is nothing more important than self-awareness. Moreover, if your parts start to drag you into mechanical sleep, I will create conditions that will prevent you from coming here. I will do it not because I want to get rid of you or take a revenge on you, even though that's what your mind will think. No, nothing of the sort. I am performing a certain operation because of which you will either understand what we discuss, or these parts will drag you back to mechanical sleep.

I have said many times that we are not here to have a nice conversation. I am not here to tell you that everything is great with you. We are here for something quite the opposite. I start to show you certain parts of you that you must bring to the surface and become aware of. You are the only one who can become aware of what's going on with you. My task is to create opportunities for this to happen. I cannot become aware for anyone except myself, but I can create opportunities that increase the intensity of the process of awareness of those in a group. That's why our Process is accompanied by an increase in excitation that continues to escalate. We can only see what's inside us when the voltage is high.

We have already discussed that we can only investigate ourselves by looking inside ourselves. A human being consists of many different parts. Many people acknowledge that, but few see how these parts work. To see these parts, you should manifest the clash of these forces inside yourself. We are dealing with one of these clashing contradictions now: I have the intention to come to the seminar, yet at the same time, I create a situation which prevents me from coming to the seminar. This is the work of your opposing parts. They have their own notion about which things are more important, and how you to lead your life.

I repeat, I do everything I can to make you understand that nothing is more important than this Process. I am not talking about myself or the School of Holistic Psychology—this is just the form in which the Process expresses itself. **The Process is self-awareness.** I want to repeat that the impulse toward self-awareness very rarely manifests itself in people at the present time.

From my point of view, any system that aspires to call itself spiritual should work with awareness. Without awareness, a system is not spiritual. The impulse of self-awareness enters this density of consciousness, but it is being perceived very weakly by human civilization.

Where does the impulse for self-awareness come from?

— The physical body changes according to certain programs with which it has been downloaded. While going through its developmental stages, the physical body receives certain impulses. These impulses realize certain changes in the body. But what about self-awareness? Where does this impulse come from? There are few people here who can catch this impulse, and the number of people who can follow it as the most important thing in their life is even smaller.

Using the analogy of the caterpillar-butterfly transformation, we can say that nature provides a human being with the physical body and a dual personality. Nature is not interested in anything else. The body and personality pass through every developmental stage, from birth to death, where everything ends. Movement toward self-awareness will lead to global changes in human civilization. People do not yet understand what our Process offers, as it is just beginning.

Some people come here expecting to learn how to use teleportation and telepathy. I tell them, "Perhaps, you will get there one day, but you need to become self-aware first. Who are you? Where are you coming from? Where are you going?" You will not receive the extrasensory abilities your conditioned mind is so eager to receive here. Well, at least this will not happen during the early stages of your work.

As a result, some of you ask, "Why do I need this? And what exactly do I receive here?" Obviously, we all receive a high level of excitation here. I used to live mechanically before: I am hit—I hit back, I am condemned—I condemn in return. There was a certain pleasure in it. But we are entering something new here. **We are invited to not do things that provide us with the greatest mechanical pleasures, but to become aware of the mechanisms of the work of the conditioned mind. That's how we start to become aware of who we currently are.**

I would like to discuss what we are offered here, and why each one of you needs this.

— *My mind doesn't know what to call it, but I feel something new and unknown.*

— Some of the books of the School of Holistic Psychology address this question in detail. In using certain words and notions, I try to explain the laws on which the conditioned mind operates and point you in the direction of the exit out of the duality that gives birth to fear, fight, and suffering.

Can you discern what happens here and other so-called esoteric, religious, and psychological groups? What motivates you? Why do you think you need to be here? Are you here because of a certain habit of which you are not even aware? Everything can turn into a habit, even awareness. That's the most difficult trap of this reality. What brings you to our seminars?

— *I am driven by a wish to see the laws on which the conditioned mind opperates. I want to know how we create our fate. I am not interested in abstract things.*

— Yes, I can't imagine anything more concrete, but what I discuss is not simple. Moreover, it requires you to experience it.

Understanding what we strive toward comes only through the aware experience of your parts that you don't want to accept in yourself. To receive these experiences, you need to have certain notions that do not correspond to the notions most people share here. You must accumulate the base of knowledge and apply it in your own life—to experience it. It is only in the process of such experience that you will come to understand yourself.

It is impossible to bypass bodily changes. The time comes when a child starts to talk and walk. Certain hormonal changes occur. It is not so straight forward when we deal with the impulse of self-awareness. A human being may start to "walk" in terms of self-awareness and "talk" in terms of self-awareness, and then suddenly drop it. Interestingly, in the case of self-awareness, changes are not irreversible.

— *Do people who stop doing this work ever return?*

— Based on years of my experience with different groups, I can tell you that those who quit the Process never return. I have never kicked anyone out. People who leave do it on their own volition. It doesn't take them long time to forget everything they have learned here.

The impulse toward self-awareness is a very strong impulse. It is as strong as a child's impulse to start talking. The physical changes we can see: a child suddenly starts to talk, or a boy turns into a man. It's different here. It's not visible. It's not obvious. It's very strange, stressful, and painful.

— *I frequently wonder whether this process can be less stressful.*

— Stress or excitation appear in connection with the identification with one side of duality. When this happens, the opposite side also gets reinforced.

7

Personality expresses only one side of duality

— This is the peculiarity of personality. In the body of a human being, a dual personality gets formed, one side of which is conscious while the other is sub-conscious. Based on the self-identification of a human being with only one, conscious side of the personality, a constant inner conflict with its opposite side starts. In other words, a human being starts to fight with himself.

That's how the life of any human being, nation, or civilization can be described. Every conflict and war appears because of the dual personality structure of a human being. But this is not yet a common point of view. So, a human being has two personalities: one conscious and the other sub-conscious. They are completely opposite from one another, and they fight each other.

The mechanical, sleeping human being becomes a playground for this fight while being totally unaware of its mechanisms. We can only start to see these mechanisms, which manifest themselves in our constant fighting within ourselves, through self-awareness. I talk about this all the time using different words, but the essence of what I want to transmit to you is the same. This is an experiment for me. I don't know whether there are other people on this planet whose impulse of self-awareness is equally strong. Why do you think I need it so badly?

— *Do you need this to broaden your consciousness?*

— Yes, I need this to broaden my consciousness and to become enlightened. Those are the words, and I am not the only one who speaks these words. Those are the most common words in esoteric literature.

— *One has to say something about oneself. Not everyone can do that. And not everyone can understand ...*

— In order for me to meet a man who I can tell about myself, I first have to know something about myself. Otherwise, I can meet

8

such a man, but I will walk right by him without even seeing the opportunity that has appeared. One can only approach this situation when the impulse toward self-awareness has been born, i.e. when one starts to understand who one really is, then one can discuss it with others.

It is only at that moment that you will be able to say that, because you will have what to say. I am shifting the accent now from the external side, i.e. from a human being who you are going to say what you must say, toward you, a human being who is going to say what he must say. The main question is what are you going to say about yourself? Let's say you have such a human being—me, for example. What can you say about yourself?

— *I don't know.*

— You don't know? Here you go. You just had this opportunity, and this is the result.

This reality is not built on understanding; it is built on agreement.

— This reality is not built on understanding; it is built on agreement. People who agree on some topic get together and create groups, organizations, societies, etc. For example, a group of people share the belief that Jesus is God's son, and he came to earth to save us. Every member of this group agrees with this statement; they don't question it. They may question other statements, but not this one, with which they all agree, and based on this, they all gathered into one organization. That's how different groups, organizations, and societies get created.

— *I agree with this, but sooner or later, they will come to a point of disagreement.*

— Some confessions can exist for a very long time. There are certain postulates that express what every one of their members agree with. When people appear amongst them who disagree with these basic postulates, they either move to other organizations, or they create their own branches or even a new organization, in which postulates correspond to their notions.

A human being is a peculiar creature that must believe in something. Moreover, this belief or faith is based on certain convictions that reflect only one side of duality. In this case, convictions that reflect the opposite side of this duality will turn into something against which a man is going to fight, defending his faith.

That's the reason we see constant conflict between religious, political, economic, cultural, ethnic, moral, and other systems. I want to emphasize that these conflicts occur precisely between the organizations that express opposite views, i.e. the organizations which reflect the opposite sides of certain dualities. For example, the fight between Christianity and Islam, capitalism and communism, criminals and policemen, etc.

What happens in our Process? I don't create any kind of postulates that I would later install into people's consciousness in order to say, "Do you agree with it? If you don't agree with it—go away." Every one of you can agree or disagree here. This is the most difficult form of interaction, the interaction without rules and convictions on which the conditioned mind wants to lean.

We investigate how these rules and convictions are created in this reality. Every personality, for example, contains certain axioms, i.e. notions it sees as given and self-explanatory, as real, without any understanding that this is what it is doing. When a personality starts to doubt the righteousness of the axioms with which it was brought up, we call it loss of faith.

Every axiom is dual; it has opposite sides. Therefore, you can only believe in an axiom that expresses one side of duality while rejecting the axiom that expresses the opposite side. As the personality of a human being is dual, it contains opposite axioms simultaneously. The only question is which one of them is conscious and which subconscious.

From this point of view, the fight of the opposite sides that occurs in the external world, which nowadays happens to be the essence of all human relationships, has its roots inside the personality. Therefore, any given external fight is just a reflection of the never-ending fight that each human being fights within himself.

Why don't I understand myself?

— Do you think everything that was created in your life was created by you?

— *I do. I don't think it was created only by me. Certain things, I was led to.*

— Stop. You have just pronounced two different assertions.

— *Yes, certain things were created by me, and other things I was led to …*

— Who led you?

— *Society.*

— This is one of the most difficult moments of our work. The thought process of a human being is dual. The conditioned mind is dual: it sees itself as one part of a duality while the other part of itself it does not consider to be itself. That's why a human being cannot comprehend that **everything** that happens to him in his life, to the last millimeter, is done by himself. There is no moment in time that was not created by him.

But as his self-identification is limited by his image, which includes only half of his personality, the other half, his own other side, acts in opposition to it and creates situations in his life that his conscious side does not expect. In this case, the only thing he can do is to blame and condemn himself for the situations that appear in his life which do not correspond to his notions of how things should be.

For example, you consider yourself a healthy human being, but suddenly you get sick. What are you going to think? What is the disease a result of?

— *In my case, my disease resolved, and I still cannot sort out why.*

— Exactly. You cannot sort it out, but this is a very important question. Where did your disease come from?

— *Wrong food. Wrong water. Stress.*

— Where does stress come from?

— *I know that I am the one who is guilty for what I have.*

— You say you are guilty. Who are you guilty in front of?

— *I am guilty myself.*

— What are you guilty of? Are you guilty for getting sick?

— *Yes.*

— You condemn yourself for something you did yourself. You have a notion, "I should not get sick. But I got sick. Therefore, I am guilty."

There are two types of guilt. The first one, someone is guilty. This someone polluted the air, water, and the produce I buy at the supermarket. This someone ran his car over me and put me into a hospital. Now, I am sick, and I blame them. I say, "You brought me this disease." But I have a question: "Okay, you were hit by a car. But why were you on this intersection, at this time of a day, and in front of this particular car, and why did it hit you?" The conditioned mind will always search for the guilty party, and as a result, the guilty one will be someone else or me.

I can also say, "I was drunk. I was jay walking and run over by a car. I did not see it coming." First choice in this case would be, "This idiot was drunk. He was driving on the wrong side of a street. He did not see me." I assert that not a single event in the life of a human being occurs without him desiring it; he creates everything himself. The problem is that he doesn't understand who he is and how he creates everything he creates. Because of this misunderstanding, a

12

human being creates many illusions that are based on blame and condemnation of himself or others.

— *One day we will grow up to discern what's going on.*

— You will not grow up to discern unless you have an impulse toward self-awareness. Nature is not interested in it. Nature provided you with a good physical body, but you also received a dual personality that identifies itself with one side of a duality. What can you say about yourself as a personality?

— *I don't even know what to say.*

What can you say about yourself?

— That's why you can't say anything about yourself to someone who wants to hear you out. If I know something about myself, I will always find someone to tell it to. If, on the other hand, I don't know anything about myself, why do I need anyone if, and to whom, I don't have anything to say? Even if there are thousands of people around me, I don't have anything to say to them. You will not simply awaken from sleep and mechanical survival with time. You will not awaken from sleep and mechanical survival unless you have an impulse toward self-awareness.

We can see how the program of body development works in time. A child starts to talk at a certain age and walk at a certain age. There are certain averages that tell us when most kids start to do that. In terms of the physical body, these changes are guaranteed, but in terms of self-awareness they are not guaranteed. There is no nature-installed self-awareness program in a human being that would guarantee that you will become self-aware during your life time. Moreover, in those without the impulse of self-awareness, the sleep of consciousness just escalates with age.

Self-awareness is a universal technique by which you can see yourself holistically. This is a universal key that can open any one of your life situations. I will repeat that a man should have an impulse toward self-awareness. Nothing will happen without such an impulse. If this impulse exists, even if in a rudimentary form, you can start to nourish and develop it. If the impulse develops in such a way that your self-awareness becomes an irreversible process, you can wake up and become whole. Currently, it is very rare.

I don't know whether we have people in our groups for whom this process is currently irreversible. I know one thing only; I must see things the way they are. My aim is to see illusions as illusions. I know I have a key that will help me get out of any illusion and to see things the way they are. I use this key every day.

There are many illusions here. I know I am going to go through them and see what is happening here better and better, because I have the passion to see how this illusory reality works. I tell you about this passion. Is it important for you? Why do you need self-awareness? I tell you about things that I experience. I always lean on my own experience. As I go along, I arrive at the next level where another understanding gets born. This is the passion of self-awareness. I transmit it to you. Are you ready to be equally passionate in your own self-investigation?

Not understanding others is a consequence of not understanding oneself

— Are there people around you whom you don't understand?

— *Yes. There are many people I don't understand. I don't understand bums, serial killers…*

— Yes, there are many people I don't understand, but all of them happen to be part of humanity, which is one organism. So, why don't I understand something that happens in this organism? The only conclusion I can make is that I don't see things the way they see them. If they do something, they know why they do it. But at the same time, they don't understand you, who does not do what they do.

14

It looks like there are many people around here whom I don't understand. I keep looking, and I realize that I don't understand practically anyone around me. Then I suddenly realize that I don't understand myself. This is a very important moment to grasp. A human being who is asleep thinks that he either understands everything or just needs to read a couple more books and he will understand everything. This is not the case. It turns out that a man's ability to see is attuned in such a way that he can see only certain things while other things get totally rejected. It is precisely because I reject something that I cannot understand my own life, which encompasses all of this.

Why do things happen to me that I don't like or am afraid of? This happens for the sole reason that I don't see holistically. If I am a persistent self-investigator, I always ask myself the question, "Who am I?"

The one who I currently consider myself to be sees everything "right". But "right" means partial. And everything I don't see creates problems, which I consider to be normal when I am asleep. **I say that I determine my life myself, but at the same time, I carry a notion that the predominant number of things that appear in my life do not depend on me. Does everything depend on me or not? This is the main question.**

Am I interested in getting to know what I don't accept in myself? Why am I not whole? In this case, more questions appear: "Who am I now? How do I start to move toward becoming whole?" Most people don't ask these questions. But even if the answers are given, these answers will not be perceived by those who are not striving for self-awareness. The appearance of such a question is connected to the fact that I start to see that what I consider myself to be is highly fragmented, and as a result, my vision is very fragmented. That's the reason I cannot accept responsibility for everything that happens in my life. I cannot accept responsibility for everything that happens in my life because I don't think that everything that appears in my life is connected to me.

The script of your dream

— The questions I have touched upon point to the state a human being happens to be in while not even seeing it. In that case, a man can only do one thing—condemn and feel the blame. He needs to condemn for what he does not agree with and to feel guilty for his own condemnation, since by condemning others he condemns himself. The mechanism that works here always and everywhere is **CONDEMNATION and GUILT.** We either condemn someone and blame him, or we condemn ourselves and blame ourselves. The prize we get in this game is **SELF-PITY or EXCLUSIVITY.** I am not the same as everyone else. I am different. I am exclusive. But exclusive means excluded, i.e. lonely. And I feel self-pity. That's what every game here boils down to. I am discussing the results of my self-investigation with you. This is something I experience and understand only because I experience it. But it does not mean that it is going to become yours just because you are reading about it.

For it to become yours, you need to start to experience it and to become aware of it inside yourself. In this case, you will be fully assured that this is the way it is. As you read this book, you will start to feel that this is the truth. This is just a feeling. You are not sure of it. You have not confirmed that this is true. Unless you experience it, everything will continue to remain the same for you. Therefore, your task is not just to read this but to feel it inside yourself, for it to turn into something that you became aware of based on your own experience. The knowledge we discuss here is not abstract; it is quite concrete and relates to every aspect of life.

— *I saw one of my dualities. One part of me doesn't give a damn about anything. It just wants to stay in bed and cry tears of self-pity. Another side asks the question, "What is it that I do, and how do I do it so that later I am unhappy*

16

with the results?" This is how it is, and this is the way it is. It is very interesting to see things the way they are and to be the director of one's life.

— Are you interested in it the same way you are interested in seeing a new movie or is it a life necessity for you? What is the level of your passion for self-investigation?

— *I don't have any other interests now.*

— Since you are not interested in anything else now, do you believe that you are interested in this?

— *I have a part that doesn't give a damn about anything. I see it. I understand that movement is only possible when one sees both sides of a duality.*

— How can you get to know whether you have a passion for self-investigation or not? You have no way of knowing that. Irrespective of how many times you were to look inside, you would not understand that. You have just created a situation that can show you that. Let's look at the question of paying for this seminar. You must pay more than you normally pay, and you experience doubts: do I really need all of this? Am I ready to pay so much money for my passion? What is the strength of my passion? Or, I can think about how that I don't need to come to the seminar, and that I can receive everything I need from books. You can say, "My passion is big, but I can realize it without you."

You will not get anywhere without a correctly functioning group and regular seminars. But what will your conditioned mind say to that? It will say, "I am not quitting anything. I am just taking a timeout." But you cannot take a time out here. Not because I say so, but because I am creating an opportunity for you to understand whether you have this passion or not, and if you do have it, how powerful it is.

— *I think I am ready, but I feel tired.*

— Fatigue is an indicator that I am touching something very important which presently I don't want to see. **The degree of your readiness to self-investigation will be determined by the level of** your readiness to meet what you call feeling tired. **Resistance points to how important what we are touching now is. Will you investigate your resistance or not? That's what will show how strong your passion is.** I will exacerbate your resistance and say, "If you are not ready, make sure you *see* that you are not ready. If you want to leave—leave. I can give you a lot, but are you ready to absorb it?"

To reach the next level of your consciousness, you must have a very strong intention and to pay for it with an illusion, i.e. with money. Your intention must be strengthened. Increase in your payment for the webinar performs this function. The more you pay, the stronger your intention will be.

Death is the greatest illusion of this reality

— Recently, I activated one of my personal dualities "disease—health", and I saw my very strong identification with the physical body. **Identification is a state which prevents you from observing what you have identified with.** I saw that I have a difficult time observing painful sensations in the body. I created exacerbation in the disease to see and de-identify with this duality. My identification with this duality is connected to another key duality, "life—death". A human being forgot that he is eternal and immortal. That's why he created the world where death is real.

When a human being is dead, he starts to create death. The state of a killer, for example, is a dead state that creates death around it. When you forget that you are eternal and immortal being, death turns into a very real event. Death allows you to enter the state of the side of duality you reject. For me, disease is death.

Identification with a duality you don't accept leads you to the state of death, i.e. into the grandest illusion created by human beings. Everything else is a result of this illusion. Every war that is carried out can only be carried out in a state where death is real.

To be dead is to stop existing. A human being will create murder in such a state. Moreover, he will not be able *not* to create it. He will kill everything because he is dead. In that case, what's the difference who he kills? Every killer thinks that he will disappear. Being in such a state, they want to carry as many lives with them as they can. They want to confirm the point of view that everything is dead.

People who are alive cannot destroy life. Only dead people can destroy dead people. But those they destroy are also dead. This is the most interesting thing. An oppressor finds a victim, which believes he is going to die; death is real for him. That's how one dead human being destroys another dead human being.

— *While working in the medical field, I saw how the inner pair of a human being who happens to be in harmony, love, and unity, doesn't get attracted to the lower vibrations, such as war, earthquake, etc. It simply floats around them.*

— Exactly. Your state creates your reality. People who happen to be in the state of death create death. They are incapable of not creating it.

— *I was completely blown away by the fact that your environment will not affect you if you happen to be in a different state. This was a very unusual experience. I was in a cocoon which protected me from lower vibrations.*

— I was always amazed by the speed with which a human being can transfer into the state of being a killer. Now I understand that for someone who happens to be in a state of death and who really accepts death, it is easy. He thinks he will disappear. In this case, why not take someone with me? People are prohibited from realizing their homicidal tendencies by the law, police, and punishment. If we were to remove this prohibition, we would see people killing people left and right.

The huge number of people who happen to be in the reality of death will realize it. Currently, they are afraid of the law. If we were to remove these limiting factors, a human being would turn into a being that kills. The killing state is totally normal for such people

19

because they are dead. Most people here are dead, and dead people kill other people easily. They don't have anything to lose. For example, all mafia people are dead. The level of fear to which they are exposed is very high.

The popular killer

— By creating the illusion of death in this reality, people become totally absorbed by it. In a state of a dead man, you will commit murder. It will be impossible for you not to commit it. You will not be able to comply with the law, "Shall not kill" because you will not even understand this law. You will not have any other law but the one of the criminal court that is reinforced by punishment.

If we were to remove punishment, people would be able to kill freely. Some people try to avoid societal law. They kill and then try to hide the evidence. Others do not hide that they kill. They say, "Look at how I was treated. Why do you want me to treat people differently? I have not killed enough. If you let me go, I will continue to kill." They condemn this society. They say they were killing and would continue to kill because they cannot live any other way here.

There is one other fact that has caused me to experience a strange state. When some people discuss serial killers, they say that they liked some of them, such as Al Capone, Bonnie and Clyde, and other killers. Why? This situation reflects the state many people are currently in. They would like to do what these killers have done, but they are afraid of repercussions. Most people live in this dead state. While in such a state, a human being is simply unable not to kill other people. It is useless to talk to such people about life. They will not understand.

— *They think that the world is full of enemies and they should protect themselves. The only way for them to do it is to kill.*

— They think the world is a prison where only the strongest survive. They want to become the strongest, and the strongest are

20

those who kill without thinking twice about what they are doing. The common societal norms prohibit killing, but these people live outside the norms and say, "I killed, and I will kill." They don't have a conscience. **Conscience is a state of remorse a human being experiences for doing something that society does not accept, i.e. for breaking of the law.**

— *The laws of biology that we studied in school also talk about survival of the fittest.*

— Yes, this is precisely the law dead people follow.

— *Jail is not the only place in which this law operates. This law operates in elementary school and in the army. If you think about it, it also operates in the corporate world.*

— That's what I am saying. We are living in the reality of dead people. The ideas we are being taught in school are the ideas of dead people. We are surrounded by dead people. There are only a few alive beings around you, who have not been touched by these ideas. The one who is alive will not do what a killer does in a state of death. The one who is alive will not be affected by this; his frequency of vibration is different.

— *Each one of us went through school. Most of us graduated from college. How did we get out of it?*

— Whether you got out of it or not is a big question. **When you get out of this state of a killer completely, you start to perceive everything connected to killing as an illusion. For example, you will not be smeared by the residue of fear while watching a horror movie.** Everything we see on TV produces a residue of fear. A dead man feels the smell of death. He sees how it can happen. News programs constantly show us scenes of killing, while the news anchors remind us those killers still have not been found. They are sowing fear, because being dead, they are unable not to sow it; their state is eternal fear of death, i.e. of the illusion that was created by them. **The transfer from the state of a dead man (which we all** submerge into when we are born into this reality) into the state of being alive is not simple.

Our Process represents such a transfer. The transfer occurs through awareness of dualities. Certain personal dualities, connected to our personality, are activated in each one of us. Personality identifies with one side of a duality and starts to conflict with its opposite side. **This fight by itself is identification. Identification prevents you from seeing yourself holistically.**

— *So you turn into it.*

Self-identification "Disabled"

— Exactly. If you, for example, are identified with the duality "health—disease", you will not be able to observe it from a side. The only thing you will be able to do is to try to change your state to the side you find to be more habitual, for example, health. You will go to the doctors and take medications. That's what most people do with different levels of intensity.

One can also identify with the side "disease". Such a human turns into a disabled invalid. Look at those people: they try to extract a profit out of their disease. Disability can be quite profitable. Society has created conditions that led to the formation of a big group of disabled people.

I am pointing to the fact that self-identification of personality can occur on either side of a duality. In that case, it can occur on the side of "disease" or the side of "health". Most people fight for the healthy life style. They are self-identified with the "health" side. But they are also strongly identified with disease and are afraid of it.

There are invalids who identify themselves with a "disease", which becomes normal for them. They see and use every advantage it offers them. Other people don't see the advantages disabled people have, while they themselves see them very well. But the duality these two groups of people activate is the same.

22

— *Healthy people are afraid to lose their health, while the disabled do not want to part with their disabilities. Otherwise, they would lose all the perks that help them to survive: subsidized housing and utilities, free health services, and incredible self-pity.*

— *By giving an inner agreement to a "disease", a human being receives this particular disease and all the perks connected to it.*

— *On one side, he happens to be in a state of disability, self-pity, but on the other side, he plays this game very well, to the point of bravery.*

— I have recently felt this state of disability myself. The disabled one does not ask but insists, "I am disabled. Step aside. Let me through!" He gets irritated if people don't notice him and don't do what he requests them to do. Disabled people have their own "disabled" pride; they are fighting for the "right" cause. They carry a high level of condemnation for healthy people who consider them defective.

— *Most disabled people live out of the state of "people owe me everything".*

— *Healthy people are afraid to lose the level of freedom they have. For example, the freedom of movement and financial independence that they have based on their health.*

— The disabled one also has something he is afraid to lose.

— *The disabled man doesn't look for equality with a healthy man; he is interested in the state of being defective and in the state of pity. He is interested in being lower than others, as it helps him to survive.*

— Disabled people strongly condemn healthy people for what they do.

— *And based on this, those who are healthy consider themselves guilty in front of them.*

— From the position of disabled people, healthy people are guilty of being healthy. Consider the very interesting interplay of this duality. Those who are healthy are afraid of the disease; every mention of it is unpleasant. People live in constant fear. This is what it means to be identified with a duality: you cannot even separate yourself from it.

We are touching upon different dualities and de-identifying with them. If you are de-identified with the duality "health—disease", you can observe the paly of its opposite sides inside you.

How duality works

— The acquisition of human experience occurs through this stretching of the opposite sides of different dualities: they become more strongly expressed. I call this process activation of dualities. For example, when the duality "health—disease" is stretched, you will get sick frequently, while when the duality "smart—stupid" is stretched, you will be bothered about whether you are smart or stupid.

Activation of a duality occurs through conscious identification with one of its sides and subconscious identification with its opposite side. Consciously, personality considers itself to be only one side of a duality. For example, the personality that consciously considers itself successful will fear its opposite subconscious side— unsuccessful.

Activation of a duality brings up an increase in the intensity of excitation between its opposite sides, which is experienced as fear and leads to the escalation of conflict between its two opposite sides. This is the inner fight with yourself that every personality experiences because it is dual. Activation of a duality leads to an increase in the amplitude of its fluctuations, i.e. a human being starts to increase the physical realization of both sides of the duality of his personality. The life of such a human being becomes very dramatic. It's precisely this drama that may push him to become aware of what is really happening to him.

Only by becoming aware of the dual nature of his personality can a human being get to the higher level of consciousness out of which it can observe the interplay of the dualities of his personality. That's how de-identification with the old, mechanical notion of oneself occurs. That's how the process of liberation from the illusions of given reality occurs. Our process occurs through experience and seeing different dualities that form the character of our personality inside us.

You must understand the basic law upon which every duality works. When this knowledge starts to enter you, you have an opportunity to start to become aware of yourself. **If you don't know about the dual make-up of this reality and of your personality, you cannot become aware of yourself; you cannot see yourself the way you are now.** Many practices and theories available today do not invite you to see yourself fully, because each one of them invites you to work on only one duality. **We are setting a new goal for ourselves here: to exit out of all dualities of the conditioned mind.**

To exit out of all dualities of given reality, you must have the knowledge that will allow you to do that and to realize it inside yourself through your own experience. That's what our work is about. We are pulling ourselves out of the illusory reality. Do you remember Munchausen who pulled himself out of the wetland by pulling on his hair? The conditioned mind cannot think in terms of duality; it can only see things from one side. We must exit the borders of one-sided thought processes and enter the new, paradoxical thought process by increasing the level of vibration of our own consciousness.

From disease to health and back

— *I used to be very healthy and very active in many sports. Then I got traumatized and became a disabled invalid. It's a scary process. You are torn from the world. Everyone pities you. I did not want to remain an invalid. But how can one transfer oneself to a state when one is not bothered whether he is healthy or sick, especially when one deals with physical pain?*

— This is a very difficult moment. When being identified with the duality "health—disease", I start to activate disease, I turn into an invalid, get scared of it, and start to do everything to become so-called healthy. When I get healthy, I start to experience the fear of disability again. You must accept both sides as two sides of one coin.

Let's say my health is poor. I am hurting all over. I saw that by identifying with the state of my body, I do everything I can to transfer it to the state of health. But my fear of the disease remains in me, nevertheless, and this fear creates a chronic disease. That's what I have experienced. I used to feel like I am an old man. I could barely walk, even though I did not exhibit any external signs of disease. I felt totally empty inside. Everything bored me. I could not feel pleasure. This reality appeared to very depressive. My body stopped listening to me. I was getting easily tired and had to rest for long periods of time. My back was constantly in pain. This was not an acute state but chronic. I was constantly reminded that I was sick.

I couldn't understand what was going on because I hadn't fully explored the duality "health—disease". I used to be frequently sick as a child, and this caused me to have a very strong impulse to be healthy. I started to go to the gym daily, and I continue to do that. It is very important for me to go to the gym regularly, as physical activity allows me to transfer from the state of disease to the state of health. I go to the gym to transfer myself to the state of health. This impulse is very strong in me. I exercise and swim daily. If I miss a day, I get into a very unpleasant state—the state of the disease starts to pinch me.

— *I am dealing with the same thing.*

— We are reviewing the same mechanism. It cannot be otherwise. That's what I discuss now. I can see that your minds cannot comprehend that yet. We can talk about it from dusk until

26

dawn, but the conditioned mind doesn't want to understand it; it perceives everything on its own accord—in separation.

— *I can't get it.*

— That's right. You cannot get it. Your mind is totally identified with this duality. If the mind, seeing duality, starts to think, it means it get out of itself. You need to be a passionate self-investigator to do that. I provide you with the tools necessary for self-awareness, but whether you use them or not is for you to decide. I am telling you about the duality "health—disease". But how can you understand it? You can only come to understand it if you understand the laws duality works upon. Then you will have to experience this knowledge and come to understand everything we discuss through your own personality.

Our Process is not strictly mental; it unites the physical body, the mind, and the Soul. We are dealing with a trinity here. The information about how things are to happen here comes from the Soul. Situations that happen to you are created by your mind. Your physical body experiences them. But the human being was torn from the Soul and got into the duality of personality and the conditioned mind. It's the dual personality that creates diseases. The human body is a perfect machine that, notwithstanding the horrific treatment it gets, lives an average of 60-70 years. Our body is built to last many hundreds of years. Diseases arise because personality accentuates one side of duality while being afraid of and fighting against its opposite side. Any disease is a result of a constant inner conflict or resistance of one part of your personality to another part of it. This conflict manifests itself in the body: diseases of the organs are connected to this conflict. This is not a traditional medicine point of view. The allopathic medicine sees the body purely from physiologic perspective. Our work is different. We investigate how the conditioned mind, which cannot see duality, operates.

— It looks like if the mind were to accept this point of view, it would go crazy.

— Yes. Everyone human being who happens to be in the third density of consciousness is afraid of death or going crazy. When we get in touch with this knowledge, personality gets scared of going crazy. Clear vision activates the fear of death, the biggest illusion of this reality. One can only de-identify with the illusion of death by becoming totally aware of one's own illusory personality.

CHAPTER 2

WHO IS THE WINNER IN THE FIGHT WITH HIMSELF?

•◆•◆•◆•◆•◆•◆•◆•◆•◆•◆•◆•◆•◆•◆•◆•◆•◆•

Who will win if your right hand triumphs over your left hand?

— The most important thing for us is to understand the law on which the conditioned mind operates. The mind operates based on duality. As a result, our personality is also dual. Unless we understand that, we can't move forward. If you could absorb that, you would start to observe the dualities of your personality.

Awareness is seeing the work of the conditioned mind and dual personality from the point of view of a neutral observer, who happens to be your Supreme "I". While in the mind, you cannot see yourself, but there is an opportunity to exit to the Observer and to start to see how your mind works out of the Observer. In observing the mind, you start to see the dualities activated by your personality. That provides you with an opportunity to experience their opposite sides as two sides of one coin.

For example, I just reviewed the duality "health—disease" with you. This is one of the dualities my personality activated, and which I, through observation, activated in order to investigate. This is a very important moment that I know I must approach. Otherwise, one can experience the same thing thousands of times without becoming aware of it. That's what people do here all the time.

They relive and re-experience the same situation while being completely identified with a certain scenario which they cannot exit.

29

The conditioned mind is an enclosed space in which you will continue to perform oscillating movements from one side of it to the other and back.

— *Yes, that is what it is.*

— By having correct knowledge, you can start to become aware of the duality as the basic principle of work of the conditioned mind and personality.

You cannot become aware of all dualities at once. Only slow and methodic investigation will lead you to see how they interact and to sort out the basic pattern of their manifestation in your life.

For example, in the process of my self-investigation, I discovered that everyone in this reality is playing a part in the dramatic shows in which the actors happen to be in one of two states: condemnation and guilt. Condemnation and guilt are the manifestation of man's fear, which is born by the dual nature of his personality, the personality he is not aware of because he is totally identified with it. You must investigate yourself and explore the laws on which this duality operates. This is what we do. When you come to understand these laws, you will start to correctly see the situations of your life, which you currently cannot comprehend.

What happens to me? How can I understand this? How can I sort all of this out? Some people say one thing; others say something totally opposite. It is total chaos. It's precisely because of this chaos in people's heads that they cannot see anything clearly. This is a typical state of the average human being who comes up with slogans without understanding what is behind them. Some turn into fanatics of a certain point of view and start to oppress others with it. Nothing will happen unless you understand the basic laws we discuss. **Self-investigation should be conducted in the correct direction, i.e. the direction that will allow you to clearly see what you happen to be in.**

— Based on your example with the duality "health—disease", we can use the disease state for self-investigation; instead of mechanically living through a disease, we can use it to investigate ourselves. We should not run away from it. We should consciously enter it and try to see what kind of important information the disease carries.

The correct self-investigation

— You come to know God when you know God. This is the paradox mystics talk about. Concerning self-investigation, we can say that self-understanding appears when you come to know yourself correctly. Everything I create in my life is a script of my personage in this reality. By investigating this script, I deepen my understanding of the laws of a given reality.

— I have created a disease. Now, I will sort out why I created it.

— You have to investigate this question based on the knowledge of duality of your personality. When you start to see it this way, you will start to correctly understand why and how you create something in your life. This deals with duality, which is the base upon which this reality functions. You must see which duality of your personality you have activated. The conditioned mind doesn't want to see it, since in that case, it will be declassified. It does not want this to happen. **The conditioned mind prevents you from seeing its conditionality; it will try to avoid it at all costs.**

— Let's take a negative emotion. Let's say irritation. Who said that it is negative? It can lead us to duality.

— You are right, but I constantly push you to take the next step. Using my own example, I just showed you how to approach and investigate duality. I activate the duality "health—disease" in myself. Then, I experience and exit it using awareness, i.e. I start to see clearly what I was identified with.

As a self-investigator, I can start to investigate another topic only once I've solved the one I have been working on. You should not grab too many topics at once. You pick up a topic and you work on it; when you are done, you take another one. I have been talking about the topic I was investigating recently — "health—disease".

Get to know the theme of your life

— What does it mean to pick up a theme for self-investigation? It means to live through the experience of a certain duality with awareness. However, it would be a mistake to think that you can pick and choose whatever you'd like to investigate. The topics of your self-investigation have already been assigned to you. All these topics create the structure of your personality. The context and peculiarities of the manifestation of the dualities of your personality are determined by the peculiarities of its formation, which are specific for every human being. There are no similar personalities. Every personality is unique. That's why you cannot come to know the programs of your personality without conducting your own self-investigation.

I transmit the main principles according to which self-investigation is to be conducted. I also share the results of my own self-investigation with you. The results we discuss deal with the basic principles of the buildup and function of the programs of the old matrix, upon which every personality operates. I also motivate you to conduct your own self-investigation by showing how to do it using your own examples. By conducting your own self-investigation, you create and strengthen your own self-investigator. This is the most important element of our work. You must conduct your own self-investigation. I just showed you how to do that.

We can call our Process the college of self-investigation. Every student here investigates his own theme, i.e. his own personality. At the same time, we all investigate the programs of the old matrix of dual perception, which is built on fear and separation.

While living through the experience of your personality in full awareness, you'll start to understand that you create everything you have in life needed to investigate yourself. Sometimes the experience through which you are living overwhelms you like a huge wave. You submerge into the habitual for you state of identification. If your self-investigator is not strong enough yet, you can fall asleep, i.e. stop the process of self-investigation. It is precisely at those times that you need the support of someone who is awake, or a group of self-investigators.

To de-identify with your states, you must have direct mirrors. You must speak your states through without concealing anything, irrespective of what it is. You should do it with someone who also self-investigates, because the "sleeping" human being will only support your old programs, as he is identified with them. You need to have a human being who will serve as a direct mirror, who will accept what you say and return it to you without adding anything of his own. In that case, you will start to see what you manifest. You could not see it before. You were simply identified with it.

— Is this what the process of self-investigation is about?

— Yes. You start to fully express your state by carefully observing it at the same time. When you investigate the most difficult themes for you, you should have a high level of awareness, because any given theme represents a certain identification which is expressed by a difficult state of being bored and tired by everything. The only way to get out of this state is through observation, supplemented by talking it through and carefully listening to what you say.

The process of self-awareness presupposes the presence of people who will give you feedback. They will provide you with an opportunity to hear what you say to other people, i.e. to yourself. You need to understand that what you say to other people, you say to yourself and only to yourself. By talking to other people, you communicate with yourself. One part of you

talks to another part of you. This type of vision is unknown to a "sleeping" man, who thinks "I am me, while other people are other people." Until you understand that there are no other people besides you, you will not be able to conduct self-investigation.

— *It follows that the state a disabled invalid is in is a state in which everyone owes you something. Healthy people should be running around you all the time. It is a state of a small child who screams and throws tantrums demanding to be served. This state comes from childhood.*

— Yes. I saw that in my case this state is connected to my grandmother who was taking care of me. She lived with a very strong fear. For the last fourteen years of her life, she wouldn't leave her apartment, saying that she did not look good. She needed me sick. That was the only way for her to take care of me. When I was healthy, I was playing outside from early morning to midnight. I was not home, and she could neither take care of me nor manifest her love. So, she became interested in my sickness.

She used to tell me, "Don't do this. Don't do that. Don't go there." In turn, I started to manifest the opposite side, by doing everything I was forbidden to do. I would stretch this duality very far. She was saying, "Get sick. Stay in bed. I will take care of you." I, on the other hand, manifested the opposite side: "I don't need you to take care of me. I'll become healthy and independent." I manifested this side consciously all the time.

— *She insisted on one thing, and you insisted on another thing. Both sides of the duality were activated.*

— The self-identification of my personality is with the side "health". At the time, my notion of health was strongly tied to the notion of freedom. The duality "freedom—not freedom" is one of the most activated dualities in the structure of my personality.

I was a sickly child susceptible to many diseases. That led me to explore different sports. My personality eventually identified with health on the conscious level. I associated disease with imprisonment and old age. I want to emphasize that my grandmother was an old woman who locked herself in a stuffy apartment as if in a prison. Those were the peculiarities of the formation of my personality. On one side: old age, fear of death, lack of freedom, and disease. My personality consciously took the side opposite to these notions, but the other subconscious side constantly created them because it was equally strong.

Lately, I have felt like an old man who, tired of everything, does not see any meaning in this reality. This state is totally opposite to the state in which I conduct my seminars—the state of very powerful spiritual uplifting. Until I became aware of this duality, these fluctuations were very strong and frequent.

This process is very time consuming. Certain dualities, especially those with which we get inculcated in childhood, get activated very intensively. You experience them repeatedly, and at a certain moment you start to clearly see both sides of them. That allows you to de-identify with them.

The first moment of my becoming aware of this duality was in seeing that my feeling myself as an old, tired man is opposite to the excited state in which I conduct my seminars. This early vision started my work on this theme. I totally see it now with every attribute of old age, disease, and fear of trauma. To become aware of a certain personal duality, you need to acquire the experience of the wide diapason of states connected with the opposite dual sides of the duality, and to become fully aware of this experience.

When duality is ripe, you can open it

— It is not easy to allow a fruit of duality to ripen. For a human being who grows such fruits of dualities, to become aware of them is hard. I just showed you how I do it. When duality opens itself, you see both sides of it clearly and in detail.

Previously, I did not think my grandmother played such an important role in my life. I can see now how big of a role she played in the activation of the duality "health—disease" in my personality.

To conduct self-investigation, you should have a tremendous passion for it, be ready to stretch dualities to their limits and know the laws on which they operate.

— *When one enters a duality, one must constantly observe one's reactions and to not identify with it.*

— *I used to avoid everything I did not like. I used to run away from myself.*

— *This is the normal state of a "sleeping" human being.*

— Grow to love your enemy. I used to see disease and connect to it old age, traumas, and death as an enemy. Therefore, the conscious side of my personality did not want to see it. But it constantly interacted with it anyway. Right now, disease manifested itself in my body in the form of furuncles that are constantly in front of my eyes. Only once I understood that I had created it myself did I start to investigate its causes.

I could have blamed the human being who contributed to the appearance of this disease, but I understand that I attracted this human being into my life myself. If I don't have a full understanding, I will scream, yell, and condemn another human being for making a mistake. A "sleeping" man will always find someone to blame when things go not the way he thinks they should go. An aware human being doesn't blame or condemn anyone. He searches for duality which stands behind his problems with the intention of exploring it and discovering the mechanism of its action.

The conditioned mind cannot comprehend what awareness is about. You cannot become aware of anything by using the mind. Irrespective of how well I talk about awareness, the "sleeping" man will not understand me. It's imperative for our Process to select people whose ability to self-investigate starts to open. When this ability opens, they start to see the dual perception of their personality and see the events that they are involved in from the position of duality. They start to absorb and implement the idea that everything that happens in their life is created by them.

Nothing will happen without it, as you will continue to blame and condemn other people, simultaneously feeling guilty for why you condemn them. Nothing in life happens outside of a human being. If he understands that, he starts to work on figuring out what exactly he creates in his life. He becomes interested in how he creates his life. Why do certain situations that happen to him scare him? Why does he want to run away from these situations? If he remembers that he is the one who created these situations, he receives the opportunity to understand the dual nature of his personality.

He starts to see that identification of his personality with one side of the duality leads him to fight its opposite side. He starts to understand that so-called negative events represent the creation of another side of his own personality. Slowly but surely, he starts to understand that he should stop this fight that occurs inside his personality, accept the opposite side of the duality by seeing himself in it, and come to love it. This is the road toward one's wholeness.

From the point of view of the personal characteristic "I am strong and healthy", the characteristic "I am sick and weak" is an enemy. Everything here is built on the endless struggle between the opposite sides of personal dualities. The function of this struggle is to extend and activate the opposite sides of the dualities, i.e. the stronger your fight with yourself in the image of the external enemy, the stronger you activate certain personal dualities and accumulate the experience.

Such a mechanism works automatically, and most people lack the ability to understand it on the level of awareness. Subconsciously, every personality is looking for people and situations that will activate dualities that have been inculcated in it. For example, people in whom the duality "faith—no faith" is activated will search for religious organizations. Obviously, they will always suffer, even though from the point of view of one part of their personality, they are moving toward faith. But at the same time, their faith leans on its subconscious opposite part, i.e. on lack of faith. Their faith is fighting their side which doesn't believe. This fight creates suffering.

It's impossible not to suffer here because human beings fight with themselves. When a human being starts to see the mechanisms of the work of dualities, he will receive a real opportunity to get rid of suffering by stopping the inner fight of the opposite sides of his personality. It was in relationship to this type of inner war that Jesus said, "Love your enemy." A "sleeping" man doesn't see or understand this. He is searching for salvation in the outside world while it is inside him.

What does the dead one feel?

— *As a dead man, he doesn't feel anything.*

— We can't say that dead people don't feel. The feeling they experience is fear, and they feel it quite strongly. Fear transforms into different emotional states, which can be narrowed down to condemnation and guilt. They experience fear, and they start to look for a scape goat that they can condemn for the fear they experience.

Why am I scared, and because of whom am I scared? This is the basic question "sleepers" have. The conditioned mind objectifies its fear, explaining it in terms that are habitual for it, and then it finds the guilty one to condemn. That's why the victim—oppressor game is so widespread here. The oppressor tends to condemn someone, while the victim tends to condemn itself. The oppressor finds a victim, and they play out a show in which everyone receives what he needs. This is what happens on the individual level as well as on the level of organizations, nations, and countries. The mechanism of the realization of such a drama is identical in every case.

A guilty party must be found whenever people experience strong fear. Let's consider our resent history. Stalin condemned and prosecuted millions of individuals and groups of people. He masterfully orchestrated many shows condemning enemies of the people. The level of fear in the USSR and in Stalin himself was enormous. He saw threats and enemies everywhere. That fear has been objectified. To do that, you need to find the enemies of the people, i.e. enemies of Stalin. These enemies, i.e. personalities in a state of victimhood, were easily found. There were many such people in the USSR, as victimhood is a Russian national quality. Many such people were physically exterminated. "When you get rid of a human being, you get rid of the problem," Stalin used to say. But the problem is not in another human being, it's in one's own personality.

— *Do worry, anxiety, irritation, and grudges represent different types of fear?*

— Yes. The "sleeping" man lives in fear. He doesn't know anything else. When the level of fear max outs, he kills other people, thinking he can get rid of his fear that way. Killing comes natural to a dead man: you will either kill or you will be killed. This is the principle of war. That's what soldiers are taught. It's not easy to deal with this level of consciousness. The dead man believes that people want to kill him, and as a result, he is always ready to shoot first. This perception is widely popularized by mass media. In watching movies, TV shows, and news, people receive an impulse of fear. "This can happen to me," they think. That's how fear is reinforced and transmitted.

How the hysteria of war is created

— How is the hysteria of war created? Propaganda creates an image of an enemy. That's what Soviet propaganda did in respect to capitalism. Those who are in fear need a visible enemy. It is very easy to start a war because everyone here lives in fear. When the level of a country's inner fear goes overboard, it must be dumped outside. The search for the external enemy starts in order for this fear not to burst the country from the inside. When an enemy is found, war is declared. This is a common scenario.

— *When the level of fear becomes colossal, a dictator rises to power..*

— Yes. He will reflect the "will" of the people. Germany would not have been able to do what it did if most of Germans did not share Hitler's views. The same thing happened in Russia, Italy, and Japan. When an oppressor appears, a victim salutes it.

— *The level of oppression in the USSR was very high during Stalin's reign. Two major oppressors started WWII.*

— Exactly. The level of inner tension of fear in the USSR was colossal. The external enemy was needed as otherwise the country would have burst from the inside. Stalin and Hitler created a tandem. Hitler was Stalin's embodied fear, while Stalin embodied Hitler's fear. The entire political map of the world represented victims and oppressors.

We tend to hang every mistake on Stalin nowadays, but this is not only about Stalin. People were living in a state of total fear prior to the war. At the same time, slogans such as "Long live Stalin!" and "Long live motherland!" were proclaimed all over the country. Few people allowed themselves to see things differently than the way country's political leaders saw them. Those who did were isolated and exterminated. Most people were deaf and blind to any contrary information. The instrument of fear was used full force to suppress the opposite side.

— *The history of the Earth is the history of wars.*

— Yes, our perception of the world is connected with the history of wars. There is a pattern here. The same laws operate on the level of the individual human being and on the level of civilization. The way civilization exists depends on the way the personalities it is made of exist.

Nations that have their own peculiar characteristics are big egos made of personalities, i.e. small egos. Two nations at war represent two egos that project their subconscious sides onto each other. One ego relates to another ego as to something that can destroy it. The mechanism of the relationship between the nations is the same as the mechanism of the relationship between personalities.

If I were to discuss history, I would discuss it from the point of view of duality, as war is the external manifestation of the inner war that occurs between opposite sides of dualities. Many books have been written on the topic, but none of them views it from this angle. These books review multiple details of different wars without seeing the basic mechanism of dual contradictions. This is a characteristic of the conditioned mind, which is not capable of seeing itself. The mind is not capable of thinking in duality; it simply realizes mechanically the paradox of interactions of the opposite sides of dualities. The same can be said about any other product of culture, religion, economy, or politics.

Distrustful trust or the duality "faith—lack of faith"

— *The duality "trust—distrust" was strongly activated in me. I am currently experiencing severe distrust in my life, i.e. no one around me can understand me.*

— What do you mean when you say, "No one can understand me"?

— *I don't understand myself.*

— So, one half of you doesn't understand the other half of you.

— *I don't have faith.*

— One side of you has a certain faith, while the other side has an opposite faith. But the faith of one half is perceived by the other half as a lack of faith. Look at it from the standpoint of duality. Personality is made in such a way that one half of it will believe in something that the opposite side will not believe in. Therefore, you can only find the ground you can lean on in awareness, which is outside of trust—distrust, belief—disbelief, faith-faithlessness. It just observes both sides of duality, understanding the law of the unity of opposite sides. An "intention" produced by one side of the personality is not an intention but a desire; the opposite side will have the opposite desire in equal strength.

— *They are equaly strong in my case.*

— That's how it should be. Which side are you speaking about of when you say, "I don't have the money"?

— *I am speaking out of the side that doesn't have faith.*

— That's correct. This side doesn't have the money because it doesn't believe in the importance of the seminar. "All of this is irrelevant, and I will not pay money for it," it asserts. The opposite side says, "This seminar is very important to me, and I have the money to pay for it." You can only exit duality by accepting both sides of it in yourself, as they are necessary for each other. To exit the borders of duality and to create an intention that is outside "I want" and "I don't want" is a decisive step. To take this step, you need to clearly see the two opposite parts of you as two sides of one coin.

— *They have been activated strongly over the last three months.*

— Vision always comes through the painful process of exacerbation in contradictions.

— *A very powerful fight occurs inside me.*

— It will continue until you start to see duality from the state of awareness. Then you will understand that this is a lawful pattern; it should happen this way.

— *Yes, everything is right. I just can't see it this way.*

— Which "you" cannot see it? This is the question. One side of you, which has saved up the money, says, "I see everything. I need to go to the seminar." The other side, which doesn't want to pay, says, "I see everything too. I don't need to go to the seminar." You start to move rapidly from one side to the other and back again. This is what people call craziness.

— *So, where is the exit out of it?*

— You will see the exit. I simply describe things the way they are here. The basic question is "WHO ARE YOU?"

— *I am a Creator.*

— You are a Creator who creates one step toward the seminar and the next step away from the seminar. You are a Creator who is not aware of himself. Those are the Creators I deal with all the time here. This is the position of a human being who happens to be in the dual, conditioned mind. This is a very good illustration. Being in the conditioned mind, you can only be conscious of one part of your personal duality, which will fight against your other, opposite, subconscious side. This fight is eternal.

The part that provides money for the seminar fights the part that ignores the seminar. This fight totally absorbs them. You become identified with one of these sides for a certain period, and then you identify with the opposite side. You fluctuate from side to side at such a high frequency that you cannot understand who you really are. If you remain in the conditioned mind, you will always be torn because you will identify with and flip from one side to the other all the time. And their fighting will not get better; it will only get worst.

But this situation offers an opportunity to exit the duality and become aware of yourself holistically. Awareness allows us to see the fight of dualities. The mind prevents us from seeing it. It is constantly confused, because that is how it is created. "Yes" fights "no", while "no" fights "yes".

— *I can clearly see this war inside me now.*

43

— Understanding differs from knowledge; it is not just a mental process. "Give me a definition and I will say that I know it." No. You must live through and experience duality. Only then you will come to understand and become aware of it. Awareness is a result of the addition of knowledge, feelings, and actions. Until you arrive at awareness, you will not understand what I say. You do not have a result in your life. When such a result is obtained, you will realize how much was achieved. I do everything I can. Whether the seed will grow or not depends on the seed, i.e. on a human being himself.

I want you to discern between what happens here and what happens in other places. Certain things must be different; it cannot be otherwise. If a man says, "This is all the same," my reply would be, "You simply don't understand. Even if awareness is present there, how are people brought to it?"

Only a master can discern how two masters bring students to awareness. It is said that a Sufi is never directed by anything except his intention, which might appear to be quite weird to the onlooker. This is true. A Sufi will never ask what to do or how to do it, because he comes out of his own vision. He forms an intention and then creates a situation to realize his intention. He never doubts regarding what he does.

Profitable sides of poverty

— How do you create the state when you cannot pay for something that you say happens to be very important for you, in this particular case, our seminar? Why does the state of poverty have such a strong hold on you? It is holding you! It means you are finding something very profitable for you in this state. Until you see the beneficial sides of poverty, you will not be able to see duality standing behind it. You are facing its negative side now; you cannot pay for something that you say is very important for you. Therefore, I ask, "How did you create the situation of poverty, and what kind of profit do you receive out of this state of affairs?" Let's dramatize this duality to see it better. Let's look at it from every side and see every manifestation of it.

— *I extract self-pity out of this state.*

— *Poverty allows me to hide my laziness.*

— *In my case, poverty allows me to be irresponsible.*

— I want you to notice that poverty has its own pride. During the Soviet era, for example, the slogan "We are poor, but we are proud" was quite widespread. People were proud in comparing themselves with capitalists who would kill for a profit.

— *I saw that no one understands me because what we study here is very difficult. My mind is full of pride: everything is so tough, but I understand it. It means I am smart. A sense of inner self-importance appears, and pride follows because of it. I am poor, but I am smart.*

— It is not easy to refuse such a notion. This is the pride of your poor side. Christianity sees pride as one of the major sins and asks people to fight against it. But I haven't met a single human being who was able to overcome his pride. I only see that fighting with it increases it. Moreover, pride has many faces. So, where does it come from, and why is so persistent? We can only understand it if we explore this topic from the point of view of the dual nature of personality.

Pride appears based on the "righteous" condemnation of the conscious side of personality, of its own subconscious side. Pride appears on the grounds of condemning the interrelationship between two opposite sides of the dual personality. The conscious side of personality always considers itself to be better that the unconscious side and, as a result, condemns it. The degree or intensity of such a condemnation is what people call pride. Therefore, variations in pride are as diverse as variations of duality. Returning to our conversation about the poor part of your personality, we can say that you receive

45

satisfaction from the exacerbation of its pride. But it is precisely this pride that prevents you from letting money into your life.

— *I am poor, but I am very sensative. My heart is working very well.*

— *I am poor, and I am proud of it. I am poor, but I am honest.*

— This is great. The Socialist era brought us a notion that only a poor man can be honest. Rich men cannot be honest. No one notices that rich people frequently work eighteen-hour days and don't take a vacation for years. This is how many of us were brought up.

— *I am ashamed to have a lot of money.*

— Let's discuss the positive sides of poverty, because each positive side supports its negative side.

— *When I don't have money, I don't have problems.*

— As we can see, you do have problems.

— *When I don't have money, I am not scared of losing it, i.e. I don't attract criminal elements. I am poor, but I am not afraid to lose my riches.*

— *A few years ago, I sold my house and received a large sum of money for it. With money came a fear of being robbed and a fear of losing it due to inflation. Unable to withstand this fear, I invested into a business venture my friend invited me to take part in. It turned out not to be a successful investment. I've lost almost all my money as a result. I wound up being poor again, but now I can condemn my friend who advised me to invest with him. I have not pressed charges, and I have not gone to mafia to return my money. I am patiently waiting. I clearly feel that "I am good" with my friend playing the "bad" part on the background. I handled this situation so "well". No one else could have handled it the way I handled it.*

— *I extract another pride out of poverty. A rich man cannot survive on two thousand rubles a month, but I can. I am thrifty. I am a good housekeeper.*

— *I only see pluses in my poverty. It is thanks to being poor that I became very creative. My refrigerator is empty, but I can steel feed ten people. I live with the notion, "I don't have any money, but my kids are fed and clothed." We have everything we need, and we are okay. I survive, and I am proud of it. I am honest, and I don't steal. Rich people steal, but not me; I am a poor, law-abiding citizen.*

I am proud that my family can survive on a hundred rubles a week. No one can do that but me. I work two jobs to make ends meet, and I don't want to change anything. I am happy. I will have to get another job to attend a seminar.

— You can work three jobs and you still will not be able to get out of poverty. Money will not come to you if you persist in your notion of the positive side of poverty. You need to see its negative side too. At the end, we will have to see both sides together.

"I am unhappy, but I am proud…"

— *I am upset with myself for not being able to pay for the seminar. I feel very low: other people can pay for it, but I cannot. I am poor. I feel humiliated. I can feel the negative side of poverty very well now. There are people here who can decide to pay for me being there or not. They can decide whether I will attend this seminar or not. I feel I am being judged. They will judge whether I will be rich or not.*

— No, it's not up to them to decide that. The state of being wealthy is an inner state. It has nothing to do with somebody deciding on your behalf. You are in a state of humiliation, because others can pay for it and you cannot. This state of humiliation stresses you out, and you want to get up and leave. But you also feel that this seminar is very important to you. That makes it difficult for you to leave, even though the feeling, "I am important" leads precisely to such an outcome. That's where a strong contradiction appears: "I am unhappy, but proud." You think about yourself in this way, and these thoughts cause you to experience these states.

— *Yes, I feel overwhelmed with pride.*

— Start talking about it. When you talk about it, this state is not you anymore; otherwise, you identify with this state. To start seeing this state, you need to escalate the situation. Then you should start to talk about it with people who have similar experiences, i.e. not to condemn someone but to start to see things the way they are. As you

47

speak about your state, you de-identify with it. Currently, you are strongly identified with your state. Keep talking about it.

— *I cannot talk about it. I feel it, but I cannot say anything about it.*

— One part of you wants to speak up, but another part doesn't want to do that, because as soon as you start to talk about your state, you will define it and make it visible. That's precisely what this part wants to avoid. It wants to stay invisible. Start to discuss yourself from a side, as if you were a personage called Svetlana.

— *She stays there with her mouth shut, suppressing the scream inside. She is in pain. She is crying.*

— We are submerged in pain and fear in this reality, and we are taught to hide our feelings. Men are brought up not to show their feelings at all. Men, who are trained as warriors, cannot manifest their feelings at all. They can neither manifest nor discuss their fears. That leads to severe psychological problems.

— *I am cruel. I am very cruel. I keep a constant smile on my face. I feel bad, but I smile. I am cruel to myself, and I am cruel to other people.*

— We live in an interesting world, where we are trained to smile and not to show our pain.

— *I am afraid people will not understand me.*

— If someone were to start talking about his pain, he would be considered hysterical.

— *That's true. I feel hysterical. I want to hit my head against a wall. I want to scream, "I cannot go on like this! I've had enough!" But I cannot do that. I can't show my weakness. I should smile and pretend to be strong.*

— You experience tremendous fear, and you don't show it. This is the way to manifest power here.

— *This fear is enormous.*

— There is nothing but fear here. Every one of us lives in fear. It's considered to be an honor not to show it. That's why we lead such a strange life.

— I push this fear deep inside myself, and it transforms into agression. I live with a constant desire to hit someone and to defend myself.

We realize what we are afraid of

— By pushing fear inside and not showing it, we realize it in the physical reality. We realize what we are afraid of. Until fear is accepted as the essence of the old matrix of consciousness, and until people start to open up and discuss their fears, screaming and smearing tears on their faces, nothing new will happen. I scream and cry when I hurt. I express what I feel.

— I can express it at home, when I am alone. No one has ever seen me crying.

— You fool yourself, believing that fear is your life. In this case, you turn into a dead man and do what dead people do. The only way to get out of this state is to accept everything that is connected to this dead man state, i.e. fear, pain, condemnation, guilt, and pity. To see it, you should allow yourself to express it. Otherwise, nothing new will happen.

— I am tired of this fear. I am tired from having to constantly pretend that I am strong. I want to allow myself to be weak. I want to be a normal human being.

— A normal human being here is the one who hides his fears. What does it mean to be a "normal human being"? Do you understand what it means? These are just words, meaningless words. We need to open the abscess of fear that permeates this entire reality and see it as something that is not you. When we are born, we enter the world of duality where everything is based on separation, i.e. fear.

— We have to de-identify with everything we once identified with.

— I had another abscess excised today. I have experienced severe pain during this procedure. This pain was not only physical; it was also psychological. It was connected to my experiencing my birth here. I did not want to be born here because I knew that in being born here I would forget myself. At the same time, I knew that I would be able to preserve my ability to remember myself through very high sensitivity.

I inculcated my personage with a very high level of sensitivity in order not to forget who I really am. But this high sensitivity brings me a colossal pain. I did that to submerge into three-dimensional reality and to investigate every nuance of its illusions. To live with such a high level of sensitivity, I had to create a protective structure. I had to train my body and to protect it with strong musculature. I had to train my intellect and make it very flexible. But I could not protect my feelings. Feelings are the indicator that you cannot put a protector on, as they point to the next direction of movement toward yourself. The mental constructs of the conditioned mind are born out of the dual illusion, but feelings react to such an illusion by suffering. As a result, they push the mind to awaken from the sleep of illusions. Who are you really? You will have to search for the answer to this question inside yourself.

— I did not want to remember myself. I don't have any memory of it. I don't want to be rich and to deal with large sums of money, because in that case, I will have to think. I will have to remember things. I don't remember my childhood.

— Self-remembering occurs through the activation of dualities and by becoming aware of them. One cannot experience self-remembrance by sitting in a lotus position, meditating on one's Supreme "I", hoping to get an answer that will balance a duality. No. I create situations that spread the opposite sides of the dualities as far away as possible to see them. I share my experience with you.

If you, for example, are given a calculus puzzle without instructions or explanations how to solve it, you will not be able to solve it. First, certain rules and laws are taught in school. Then, you are given puzzles to solve to strengthen these laws and rules. I am offering you rules and laws that will help you to solve the assignments of your life. You already know how to use these rules and laws. You know how to solve these assignments. You should have a passion to do it.

— *One has to be brave to do it.*

Every suffering is based on condemnation and guilt

— I am as brave as I am cowardly. But I do and I will continue to do this work. This is not just an indicator of my bravery, because bravery is connected to cowardice. This is the indicator of my passion toward self-remembrance. Yes, I experience pain. Sometimes I don't want to experience it, but I keep doing what should be done.

— *This is scary and painful.*

— Yes, it is. There is nothing but fear and pain here. When you start touching fear, it activates, and you start to feel it very clearly. But you feel what's inside you, not something that was brought in by someone from the outside. This is what it is, it just happens to be in the chronic state. Pain is always there. You will not be able to get away from it. The question is whether you convert pain into suffering.

Pain is a fact, while suffering is the mind's interpretation of this pain based on condemnation and guilt. Therefore, it's not pain that is heavy but guilt and the sensation connected to it of a mistake and of something being done in the wrong way. We want to escape pain. We want to think that this world can be pain free. As a result, we see everything that leads to pain as a mistake, connecting it either with our own actions or with actions of other people. Consequently, we persist in our condemnation and guilt, and continue to pour salt on the wound.

— *Are you saying that pain should not necessarily lead to suffering?*

— That's correct. Pain is pain. When you are in pain, you can scream and cry. This is normal.

— *Isn't this suffering?*

— No, this is a reaction of an organism to pain. **Suffering is entering into the illusion of condemnation and guilt.** I am in pain, but I have a choice to suffer or not. For example, I could have said that the massage that led me to get sick with furunculous was a mistake. Next, I would have condemned the masseuse for giving me a massage. I could have also condemned myself for not seeing a doctor sooner. There are multiple reasons to condemn someone or to condemn yourself here that would lead to suffering, i.e. something was not done right. Everything happens the right way to open your eyes to see things the way they are.

— *So, I start to feel pain, and then I humiliate and push myself into suffering by believing I am guilty. If pain appeared, I am guilty one way or another. If pain appeared, I did something wrong and by doing it, I turned my pain into a disease and suffering.*

— Exactly. This happens because humiliation is connected to elevation. This is like a seesaw: when one side goes down, the other ascends. First, I say that I did something wrong, and then I insist that I did everything right while others did everything the wrong way. Such a swing creates suffering. This psychological seesaw cannot stop. The more it swings, the more suffering you experience. Suffering is a normal state of existence of the ego, which swings two opposite sides of itself. By doing that, it creates an illusion of its own existence. Like the ego or personality is an illusory entity, it creates an illusion of suffering, and by doing that it asserts itself as something that exists.

It is precisely through suffering that the personality asserts itself. So, the end of suffering is the end of the ego. As the ego is the only thing with which most people identify themselves, they do not need to dispose of suffering. Quite the opposite, they need to get more and more of it. This is paradoxical. On one side, the ego sees suffering as something bad and wants to get rid of it. On the other hand, it does everything to reinforce it. You cannot exit the ego unless you recall who you really are. The ego is the only self-identification of a sleeping human being; he does not have another one.

A human being is afraid to part with the ego the same way he is afraid of death, because death is the disappearance of ego, i.e. seeing it as an illusion. Every effort of a sleeping human being is directed toward strengthening his ego, i.e. maintaining the illusion of its existence. The only things that require constant support are those that cannot stand on their own. The ego requires this constant support. That's where this widespread craving of people for attention is coming from. If the ego stops receiving attention, the myth of its existence will dissipate.

You can continue to support your ego or explore the opportunity to exit out of it. Are you ready to realize this opportunity or not? One can know something in this reality without experiencing it. For example, you are reading a book from the School of Holistic psychology. You read about it and you know that dualities exist, but you do not experience them in order to become aware of them. You can simply be in them as most people are. Whether they want it or not, they experience dualities without being aware of it. But in that case, they do not understand themselves.

The essence of our process is in our knowing about dualities in us, experiencing and becoming aware of them. You become aware when you experience the correct knowledge about yourself. That's why I constantly talk about this knowledge that allows us to see why one or another experience we need to live through appears. These experiences are exacerbated so we can become aware of them.

The illusory perception of the ego that most people are in does not allow them to see the duality. As a result, they experience everything mechanically. We need to be in a state of awareness. We need to apply holistic knowledge to our dual thoughts and experiences in order to become aware of what happens to us.

On four bonds that exist between two people

— Let's return to the theme "A man and a woman". Every human being contains a man and a woman inside himself. This is our inner pair: a man and a woman. As the fight of the opposites occurs in this entire reality, it is also present in this pair. To understand the relationship between one human being and another human being (note that I did not say a man and a woman, but one human being and another human being), we need to see that we are dealing with the interrelationship of two pairs.

Every human being, irrespective of the physiological sex, contains both masculine and feminine parts.

You will not have inner harmony if your inner man and your inner woman are not developed.

And don't forget that the external reflects the internal.

We can frequently observe an interesting mix-up when a human being, having a woman's body, says, "I am a woman," or, having man's body, says, "I am a man." When they say that, neither one of them understands that they also contain the opposite parts. For example, a woman in the body of a woman may manifest herself as a man and be attracted to the inner woman of a human being in a man's body.

Such a mechanism of the interrelationship of sexes is not understood today, and that results in a serious confusion. All of you must figure out how your inner man relates to your inner woman, and what kind of relationship they are in. Most frequently, the relationship between this pair is victim—oppressor. For example, a woman in a woman's body attracts a man in a man's body. What kind of relationships are built between the man of one human being and the man of another human being, the woman of one human being and the woman of another human being, the man of one and the woman of another, the woman of one and the man of another? As you can see, we are dealing with four bonds already. This is the only way to sort out the interrelationship of the sexes.

Therefore, the questions related to what kind of an inner woman you have, who is your inner man, and what kind of relationship they are in are the basic questions you should ask yourself. Most likely their relationships can be described as a fight, because any duality you have not become aware of always manifests here in the fight of its opposite sides.

— *After everything I have learned by now, I suddenly experienced the fear of loneliness. I can clearly see now, that throughout my entire life I was creating situations that would allow me to feel lonely. I ask myself, "Why did I need that?" I think I found an answer. I was receiving exactly what I was afraid of, i.e. loneliness. This loneliness was pushing me to become independent: I built a career, obtained financial freedom, chose a husband five years younger than me. I was realizing my masculine side.*

— I want to emphasize that a man forms in the state of loneliness.

— *The fear of loneliness has disappeared lately, and I simply experience loneliness. Now I understand that I needed it to acquire the experience of being independent in order to manifest my masculine side. I received this experience in full, and now I can choose another experience, for example, the experience of unity. I don't simply know that, I feel that this is so. Thank you!*

From essence to the personage and back

— *In the process of investigating myself, I understood that I am terribly afraid of death. I am also afraid of getting sick, maimed, and disabled. I consider myself very small and petty, while the surrounding world appears to be big and threatening. On the other hand, I am also convinced of the opposite—I am immortal and powerful.*

55

— Immortality is the opposite side of death. Power is the opposite side of pettiness. You can self-identify with one or the other side, but one does not exist without the other. You can master the scale of duality only once you've accepted both of its opposite sides in yourself. Every one of us will die. The personage will play out and finish his show, i.e. die. But our essences are eternal. So, we are both mortal and immortal. We need to see both sides of this coin. When you see one side, you activate the opposite side. The better you see one side, the stronger the other side manifests itself. We need to see both sides simultaneously.

— *I suddenly felt that I live in total fear.*

— As we have discussed already, there is nothing but fear here. But at the same time, the statement that everything is love is also true.

— *When I experience the state of fear, for example for my life, I can transfer to the state of eternity by recalling that I am an eternal Essence. While in this state, I am not afraid for my life. On that level, there is no fear. But on this level, I am constantly afraid of something. I should remember myself when I am being thrown from one state to another. I should return from the state of the Essence and feel the short—sixty or eighty years—time span of human life from the state where I am an eternal Essence. In that case, I would see and appreciate the value of this life more. I will relate to it differently. Realizing that I am both at once, I will appreciate life and feel myself eternal at the same time.*

— Are you familiar with the idea of reincarnation? Buddhists think that by living this life in poverty, you may become rich in the next life. The idea of reincarnation was abolished by Christianity in exchange for the notion that we only live one life. Communists accepted the same idea.

Both concepts are valid because the personage only experiences his own life. He will play out this show, and what kind of show it will be depends on the person. If we were to insist on the idea of multiple incarnations, we would not experience this show as our only opportunity. It would be like an actor who comes to the stage thinking that he plays the same role for many years, so what is the difference how he will play it today? He gets drunk and vomits all over the stage. At the end, the entire show gets cancelled. In the multiplicity of your shows, there is only one show at a given moment that you need to play the best way you can.

— *We die and we get reborn again and again. But every rebirth is different. At one point, I was a first-grade student in elementary school. Then, I got to the second grade, etc. We just need to see and feel it.*

— When we review the life scenario with the duration of eighty years, it consists of shorter scenarios: ten years, five years, one year, one month, one day, one hour, one minute, and one second long. Every second of your life is a part of your scenario. If you play it differently now, you will change the show that follows it. But to do that, you need to be in the present moment, which is, for the mechanically living human being, practically impossible.

The personality of a human being represents a script of a given life, and because of that, life is predetermined for the personality. We can only change our personal show by de-identifying ourselves with it, i.e. with personality. By recalling who you really are, you can enter the present moment and change the script of your life.

— *You have to be harsh and flexible at the same time. That would allow us to experience the situation differently.*

— *I felt life in a state of immortality. It is also life. I cannot describe it.*

— This is life of another world. You cannot create adequate notions about another world here. Even if you could create them, you would create them out of the notions of this world. That will bring strong interference.

— *Yes. If I were to say that it looks like a banana, my mind will create its notions about that world based on the notions of banana it already has.*

Who is the witness in the marriage of the mind and the heart?

— We have to use these notions nevertheless. When Jesus was asked about God's kingdom, he talked in parables. He pushed people toward certain notions. He could not express them directly. He could only bring people to them and provide the opportunity for people to feel something. One can only understand God when one knows God.

The essence of our Process is to connect the heart and the mind. This is impossible for a man who happens to be in the state of sleep of consciousness or in the illusion, i.e. who reproduces the same feelings—feelings of condemnation and guilt. He has multiple concepts and a huge bookcase of knowledge under his belt, but they do not show how things really happen. His knowledge does not provide him with an opportunity to investigate his feelings correctly. He feels, but he doesn't know what he feels or why he feels what he feels.

I recently watched a movie called *The Brain of a Human Being* produced by the BBC. It asserts that the brain of a human being is his mind. This is not the case. The mind is present in every cell of the human body; it is just more concentrated in the brain. The function that the eye performs for the brain is analogous to the function a periscope performs for a submarine. A human being sees with his mind, i.e. he sees what is in his mind. He does not see what is real. The reality he sees is limited by the notions of his conditioned mind.

— *Hmmm, that's why they say that a man only sees what he wants to see.*

— If we were to extend that statement, he only wants to see things that are in his conditioned mind. People's understanding of the mind is currently very childish. The movie does not discuss the dual nature of the mind, even though the anatomical structure of the mind points to its dual nature. It consists of two halves that are

58

divided by a partition. Different areas of the brain are responsible for different functions of the human being. Some of these areas are downloaded with long-term programs that are responsible for mechanical changes of the organism. For example, certain hormones are secreted during puberty, leading to physiological changes and the transformation of the body.

Some of the areas of the brain are initially clean. For example, the area of the memory of impressions. Whatever happens to a human being gets recorded there. This is how the program of one's life scenario gets downloaded into this bio computer, i.e. into the mind. Multiple connections develop between the neurons of the brain. Information recorded there causes certain neurons to become interconnected. That's how a program gets downloaded. Imagine a wild forest in which paths are being cut out. Some of these paths, which are used a lot, become well-developed. You can use other paths, but when one of the paths gets well-developed, it is easier to use it. Those paths represent the deepest convictions upon which the personality gets built. The program of the formation and development of personality gets downloaded into this bio-computer by activation of certain dualities. One set of these dualities is conscious convictions of the personality while another set gets downloaded into the sub-consciousness.

— *When we start to review a question from the point of view of duality, the mind gets confused. It has certain well-developed paths, i.e. our habitual notions. But it cannot connect two opposite points of view. We are working with the mind. New connections appear. New opportunities open.*

— *My mind doesn't resist anymore. It is surprised.*

— **We neutralize the hard-wired pathways in our mind. These interconnections do not disappear completely. They just stop being so dramatic. When we become fully aware of a certain duality programmed in our brain, we remove the voltage that exists between its opposite poles. In other words,** we neutralize it or devoid it of energy. The memory of what relates to it in our life remains, but it no longer creates problems. We can say that it was demined. The problem is no longer a problem, just the memory of it remains.

— It is interesting that the mind agrees to it and is ready to use this experience.

— This represents the shift of the mind to another level of work. Self-investigation provides the transfer of your consciousness to a qualitatively different level of vibrations. In the process of doing it, your mind transfers to the higher levels of its functioning. The old program will resist these changes, but the computer itself will not. A computer will resist only as far as it identifies itself with the old program. It appears to the computer that if the program is taken out, it would cease to exist, but this is not so. When the computer understands that it existed, exists, and will exist, it will allow the opportunity to change the old programs downloaded into it. You need to thoroughly feel this state of mind. This is the super-mind.

We need to heal our inner boys and girls, because they did not disappear. They are inside us, and they want to receive what belongs to them while we continue to suppress them, playing the scripts our parents played while suppressing us when we were kids. Now we are both simultaneously: a child and an adult. When we heal our inner parts, we will be totally different beings.

— When I read your books, I frequently don't understand what's behind some of the words that you use. I sometimes must read one paragraph four or five times.

False information is fragmented information

— In order to know why you read something and understand what you are reading, you need to understand the material you are reading in terms of dualities. What dualities are you dealing with here? You should start thinking about everything in terms of duality. This is not easy to do, but you should start seeing dualities in yourself.

— *This is not easy. I read your books, but I am not sure I understand the information I read.*

— You have to start to discern what exactly you need. It is difficult for many people to discern what they need because they don't know who they really are. As a result, the direction of their interests is determined by one-sided illusions of their notions about themselves. **It is extremely important to discern what you really need from what you need while under the hypnosis of dual illusions.** That's what the work of our process builds upon. The ability to discern everything you encounter is the most important ability that is being formed in our Process. You start to discern between what you need and what you don't need based on the correct notion of yourself.

— *When I understood that I would not make it to the seminar, I realized I would not search for anything else.*

—You may *feel* a strong tendency to experience a certain inner aspect of yours. Your mind may not understand what exactly you need; your search for this inner aspect is intuitive. Such a search may express itself in your looking for certain books, people, seminars, and situations. Do that, but be aware of what is happening to you. Enter these situations in full awareness. In this case, you will be able to understand why you needed this experience.

You travel in order to receive the experience you need. Imagine a fully equipped scientific base. To conduct a certain experiment, it needs new samples of soil, for example. The investigator will explore his environment, find, and bring what he needs to the base. Your excursions to find and get what you need to conduct your self-investigation are equally important. We can see our seminars as a mobile laboratory of self-investigators. You find what you need for such an investigation in different places.

— And every one of us needs something different. What one of us needs and finds interesting may not interest the rest of us. Each one of us is free to explore …

— You can investigate anything you want here. You can enter any experience. But you are not entering it like a calf dragged on a rope. No. You enter, explore what you need to explore, and get out. When I want to learn something, I enter, explore, and leave.

—A human being who investigates himself simply goes after a certain component of himself. The most important thing for me is not to forget who I am. I should return to myself after every successful exploratory expedition. In that case, I can walk into anything I want.

— I walk into a store to buy a pair of pants, for example. I look at the pants I like. I touch and assess the material they are made of. If I like what I see and feel, I try them on. If I am satisfied with the feeling they offer me, I may buy them. If I don't feel this satisfaction, I will not by them, regardless of what a salesman says. I will feel whether I am comfortable in these pants or not. For someone who is looking at this situation from the outside, it may appear that they fit me ideally, but I feel uncomfortable.

— Moreover, this situation may drag you in; everything is real in the illusion.

There is nothing here but illusions

— We live in the world of dual illusions, and there is nothing here but illusions. Therefore, we know that whatever we enter is an illusion. But do you know that you are entering an illusion when you enter it, or not? If, when entering an illusion, you think you will find the Truth, you are asleep.

— *Quite frequently, when we get into an illusion, we don't remember that this is an illusion, while most people don't even know about that.*

— You are right. Most people don't know about that. Insisting on their belief, they scream that this is the only truth.

— *Everyone tries to prove his point in a conflict, while in reality, both sides are right on their own because they activate the opposite polarities of a duality.*

— We can see the mind of a human being as an egg that contains many capsules. One half of these capsules is in the top part of the egg and is called positive, the other half is in the lower part—it is called negative. When a man comes to understand the necessity of working in the direction of his wholeness, he starts to broaden his consciousness. To do that, he needs to meet different dualities. In our example, it is the upper and the lower parts of the capsules in the egg of his mind. He starts to create different situations to connect the opposite sides. When he works through every duality present in his mind, nothing will be hidden from him. He will become a triunal being. He will be able to act with full understanding of what he does.

While the dualities are spread to the maximum, you encounter very difficult situations which you either don't understand or understand poorly. As you come closer and closer to becoming holistically aware of your personal dualities, the situation that you encounter becomes lighter, and you see them more clearly.

— *I have entered the duality "to give—to take". My house was burglarized twice. I accepted the second burglary calmly and thanked the thieves, i.e. my own taking part. Afterwards, things started to come to me, but I was unable to identify with them as strongly as I used to. I am reviewing these situations from the position of duality, not from the old, habitual standpoint of the accusation and condemnation of myself and others.*

— A human being creates these situations himself, having his own parts acting as actors. People frequently live in the state "I need to take more." What will happen to a man who tries to inhale only?

How would he feel if you tried to do that? Try it, and you will learn it through your body.

CHAPTER 3

DEPENDENT INDEPENDENCE

•◆•◆•◆•◆•◆•◆•◆•◆•◆•◆•◆•◆•◆•◆•◆•◆•◆•◆•◆•

"As I was driving a bus, my wallet was stolen from my purse."

—*My wallet was stolen from me today on a bus. I felt it. I saw my purse open, and I saw the thief who was walking away with my wallet. My first impulse was active and masculine. I wanted to get up and to run after him. But I realized that such a move would lead me to arrive late to the seminar. My inner woman asked, "Do you really have to do that?" Someone in me answered, "No. Time is much more important for me now. I also have to experience the state of giving." I had a choice, and I made it. I am not accusing or condemning anyone. I don't feel guilty. I decided to give that money to the thief as a present. I know why I am giving. My states balanced out. The seesaw of duality stopped.*

— *I just recalled that I was always interested in poverty as a child. As a kid, I always wondered how poor, old people could survive on a small piece of rye bread a day. I remember cutting a small piece of bread into small pieces. I wanted to feel what they felt.*

— You wanted to have this experience as a child.

— *A human being is happy when he experiences pleasure, irrespective of whether it is pleasure from food, clothes, or sex. I am experiencing great pleasure being at this seminar now. I am content being here. I enjoy listening to what you and other people say. I am happy to see all of you. I am happy to understand what you say. I feel I am the way I am when I am here, without masks. I am not playing a role. I feel what I feel and say what I want to say. I am not afraid of being misunderstood or accused of something here. Outside of here—at work and at home—I constantly play certain, quite limiting roles. I cannot exit the borders of these roles. People would not understand me. People who come here are very close to me. They accept me unconditionally. That's what I feel. I find that your vibrations are very close to my vibrations. I am attracted to you. I feel a part of you. Deprived of our communication, I feel loneliness and hopelessness.*

— I feel similarly. My relatives and people who are close to me frequently don't understand me. You are close to me in spirit.

— The ties that bound us together are stronger than blood ties. These are spiritual ties. These are the ties Jesus spoke of. People who gather here share the same intention. Any role performed outside of here is just a role, whether it is a role of a son, daughter, mother, or father. Role games are always full of conflict because each one of them has its own truth. Spirit, on the other hand, does not carry conflict. It does not carry a prohibition. You are getting to know yourself. You are experiencing the great happiness of self-understanding. You love everything, because everything brings you happiness of self-understanding. Everything is useful in our work. I use everything I encounter to increase my self-awareness. That's how I connect myself.

— During these seminars we master the game of playing on the chords of our souls. Playing the chords of our souls, we touch each other's souls, and they start to vibrate in unison. Other people suddenly start to feel it.

The power of your character manifests itself in resistance

— The power of the character of the personage manifests itself in the resistance of one's conscious side to one's subconscious side. Let's review the duality "health—disease". A man who is sick attracts a lot of attention to himself. People take care of him. This is a sweet, pleasant state. But if you come to investigate this theme, you need to resist your identification with a disease. You start to resist a disease by applying strong effort to strengthen your health side. For example, a famous Russian heavy weight champion, Leonid Zhabotinsky, was born as a very sick child. He resisted diseases and made himself to be one of the strongest men on the planet. Such things occur only under very strong excitation of polarities. To accomplish an inner change, i.e. to change the polarity of sides of inner duality, you need to apply super-effort.

— *I have been disabled for a long time. Recently, I decided to choose health. I immediately felt the state of malaise I felt at the time I entered the state of the disease, but now, knowing what I am dealing with, I persevere in following my intention.*

— People who receive very intense experiences here have to receive the program of activation of dualities inculcated into their personality in a wide diapason. This is manifested through a strong conflict of one of its sides with its opposite side.

— *One finally gets to know oneself through what one is not.*

— The degree of activation of duality depends on the intensity of its manifestation. This is a long and very painful process.

— *I got up this morning and found myself full of irritation. I was unhappy with everything around me. I allowed myself to experience this state of irritation by observing and verbalizing it. My older daughter came along, and I told her about what I was experiencing. She patted my shoulder and gave me her permission: "Just experience it, Mom, just experience it…" I didn't want to talk to anyone. I was boiling with irritation inside. I decided not to project it onto anyone around me. I just observed it. Then I fell asleep. When I woke up, I was in a different state. I spent many years of my life in a state of irritation. I lived in this state for months sometimes. While sharing an apartment with my mother-in-law, I did not talk to her for six months once. What was I living in? I was living in this state of irritation. It became habitual for me. I got into it again today, but I decided not to run away from it and not to project it onto anyone around me. I started to speak it out loud. I used to hide it. I used to experience it silently. I did not know how to get out of it. Today I entered it, investigated it, and got out of it. It took me about five hours. I used to throw all of it outside. This mechanism*

67

would leave me physically and emotionally drained. For example, I knew I had to spend time with the kids, but being in that state, I only had one thought in my head: "Don't bug me!" Today I have experienced something completely different. My child was willing to share her own state with me without asking anything in return. I went to bed and had a nap. When I woke up, I was in a different state. I realized that I don't need to push myself so hard. When you discover yourself in this state, you can simply observe, speak through it, and experience it. You don't have to be stressed or anxious about it. I can observe my irritation only when I am outside of it. I have started to feel a solid ground. I see that I play this show. I can observe myself only when I am de-identified with my personage.

— When you are identified with your personage, you experience everything mechanically: "Why is this so? Why do they treat me this way?!" You get irritated by everything.

— But this irritation is being used for something, right? It is not there for nothing!

"I am not irritated by my irritation anymore ..."

— Irritation is in me. It is just in me. I used to experience it without seeing it, but now I observe it. It can be projected onto everything around me. It is in me, and I can see it now. If I can see it, I can do something about it. Pint is right, "Seeing is action!" It works. It is true. I have experienced it myself. Thank you.

— Every state can be projected outside. When you are in the state of irritation, you project it outside. The mind wants to find the reason for dissatisfaction in the external world to explain the state it is in. But the reason for this state is not outside of you, it is inside. Therefore, the best thing you can do is to observe your states at any given time.

— When I observe, my mind becomes neutralized. For example, irritation gets projected onto someone around me. I immediately understand that I have caused this state myself. A certain part of me has created this state. I find this

part, I see it, and I start to accept its creativity. This part cannot create anything else. That's why we say that it is irritated. If it was different, we would have called it differently. Now I am familiar with a part of me that used to create through me for many years. It is called "Irritation". I saw many things that it has created. This part is not bad. It is the way it is. That's it.

I want to thank everyone who happened to be around me when I was irritated for accepting me the way I was without blame or condemnation. You allowed this state to manifest itself, and your permission allowed me to become aware of it. I am grateful to you for accepting all my manifestations.

— Some people live for years in the state of irritation. They can be irritated by their husbands, wives, bosses, employees, etc. A big part of their life is spent in this state. They don't see it inside. They project it outside onto other people. Observe it and start to see that it is yours. You can do something about it only if you observe it. But you can only do it with yourself, not with your husbands, wives, children, bosses, or employees. You cannot change anyone else unless you change yourself first. Change yourself, and the world around you will change.

— *I want to share a few more observations related to irritation. I have discovered that I don't have to accept the irritation of another human being. I did not know how to do that before. I am mastering this capability now. I saw how I used to allow people to use me by using irritation. It was easy to manipulate me. I saw that if I don't accept the irritation of another human being, it returns to him. I observed how this human being tried to "hang" his irritation on somebody else. He was very uncomfortable doing that. I saw all of this very clearly as if in a movie theater.*

— The state of separation leads to dilemma: either the world is wrong and I am right, or the world is right and I am wrong.

— *When one allows himself to talk about it and to verbalize all of it, it disappears like a soap bubble.*

— Exactly. But if you are not aware of your state, you try to transfer it onto someone else.

Experiencing the duality "harshness—softness"

— I would like to share my latest self-observation. The duality "harshness—softness" got activated in me strongly. I always self-identified with the harsh side. I have started to de-identify with this harsh personage that I have been playing for many years by using self-observation. The creativity of this personage includes a commanding tone of voice, irritation, arrogant posture, and insistence on its point of view. I allowed myself to manifest softness yesterday. In talking to my son, I decided not to insist on what had to be done but to gently ask him to do something for me. He was very surprised. This approach was very unusual for him. I saw it all, and I was also surprise: "How come I could not do it before? Why did I have to be in command all these years?" I could never ask anyone for anything before. I suddenly saw that I could behave differently in the same situation by centering my behavior on a different state. Knowing my personal character traits, I suddenly saw that not only I can be harsh, but I also have softness in me. I can play many different roles. I investigated my harsh side thoroughly. Now I am interested in my soft side with its characteristics of calmness, patience, and an ability to care. I don't request anything of people anymore. I gently ask them for what I need. My family observes me. They see that something unusual is happening to me: I am becoming softer. They like that. My husband and my kids started to take care of me on their own. They don't need any prompting from me. I could see that only once I de-identified with my harshness. I used to think they owed me something. I am grateful to them now for what they do. My whole demeanor has changed. My tone of voice and my gestures have changed. Our home life was different before. They were all trained by me. They knew when to perform "Sit!" and "Go!" without my even saying a word. However, my life as the commander-in-chief was not so easy. Being in a female's body, I manifested a man. I was very uncomfortable doing that. I received that experience in full. I know it very well. I can use it if I ever need to. I feel grateful for receiving this difficult experience. By getting to know myself, both harsh and soft, I can choose the state I want to manifest based on the situation I encounter. I can move further toward getting to

know who I really am. I can be different now. I was stuck in one role for many years. I am glad to be out of it. I am very interested in me. I did not understand anything during my first seminar, but now I find it very interesting.

— To realize that I don't know myself is the first and a necessary step on my road to myself. If you don't make it, you will remain asleep. You should understand that you neither know nor understand yourself. That knowledge will allow you to move to the side of understanding.

— *It took me a long time to make this step, and it was not an easy one. When I accepted the fact that I don't know myself, I started to feel better. This process is unique and takes different lengths of time for everyone.*

— A man who is asleep does not understand himself, but he does not see that. It seems to him that he knows himself. He resembles a tram that travels in a circle. To get out of this circle or to get off the track is to see the state you are constantly in. One can spend a long time riding a tram, but it only follows the same route. Tracks are laid down for the tram, and its itinerary is defined. One can change the name of the streets or the number of the tram, but the character of its movement will remain the same. Most people try to change the number of the tram they are riding, not the character of its movement. People argue about the numbers while the tram continues to drive the same old route. They don't see that. It seems to them that by changing the number of the tram they will be able to get what they want, but this is not important. People are changing the number of the train and discuss this global event, while the essence of the situation is just the game of dualities; it is like throwing a ball from one hand to another and back.

— *I would like to discuss my investigation. I finally saw my fear of condemnation. I project it onto my mom and other people. I can see now that condemnation is the tracks of my tram. Whenever I would experience dissatisfaction as a child, Mom would condemn me for it. I was forbidden to manifest it. If I was unable to control myself and spill some of it outside, Mom was quick to punish me. I was trained to be modest and self-restrained. Feelings boiled inside me, but I did not manifest them. Later, I was proud of my ability to hide my every feeling. My mother was extremely irritable, and I was proud to be able to keep myself in check while she was flying off the handle. I felt high while she was low on the ground. I condemned her for her inability to restrain herself.*

— You have to acquire the experience of the personage of your mother, i.e. You must express what you feel. If you feel irritation, you should express it.

— *This is very difficult for me.*

— *Start to observe your son, and you will see how he expresses his states. Start to do it with him and then with your mom.*

— She is waiting for it too. She should move to another state too, but you prevent her from doing that.

— *It is extremely difficult for me to do that. I'd rather be spanked hard, but she is pushing on my weakest spot—feelings.*

— *If she were to spank you, she would feel guilty, but by pushing on your feelings, she does not feel guilty. It seems to her there is nothing to feel guilty about in such a case. She has been condemning you for years without ever being punished for it. By condemning others, a man subconsciously awaits punishment.*

— Your mother is in a similarly difficult state as you. She got stuck, and she is bursting inside. Her health shows that. Her blood pressure fluctuates and goes very high. She does not see it. Try to help her. By helping your mother, you will help yourself.

— *Moreover, she is your mother, and you will always remain a child to her irrespective of how old you are. She is habitually responsible for you. Accept this responsibility and tell her about that. Free her of this responsibility. I am telling you about my own experience with my mom. It was not easy, but I did that. We both feel relief now. You should do that.*

— You have to understand that this will make her feel better. This will free her.

— *You happen to live in the state of "daughter who is not loved".*

— This is true. This is the habitual state I experience when with Mom. She does not like anything I do.

— Add the opposite experience of "daughter who is loved" to the experience of "daughter who is not loved". Open it up. This is another side of a coin. We don't destroy anything. We compliment one side of our experience by manifesting its opposite side. We are just exchanging the roles. That allows us to master the entire diapason of a duality.

— In order to feel harmony, one must manifest both sides of the duality.

— I am scared.

Love—connection of inner separation

— Behind fear is separation. You are walking toward Unconditional Love now. **To manifest Unconditional Love toward yourself means to connect your inner dually-separated parts.** To exit separation, you must de-identify with the roles you perform and become aware of their scenarios at the base of which lies the conflict of the opposite parts of the personality. Everything is quite simple. There are two opposite parts of personality. One of them happens to be on a conscious level while the other is on a subconscious level. Their interaction is analogous to the swinging of a seesaw: one on top, the other on the bottom. To become aware of the whole experience of the duality, you should consciously experience both of its sides and become aware of their unity.

— Sometimes a lighter version can work. You can simply tell your opposite side, expressed in another human being, what you feel and invited him to feel you. If that doesn't work, you should move to the level of physical action.

— In your case, it will be very important to manifest your state in action. How will your mother react to it? She will react the way she will react. Remember, you are not doing it for her. You are doing it for yourself. We cannot do anything for other people. We can only create opportunities for them to do something. Whether your mother

73

uses this opportunity or not depends on her, but you have created this opportunity for yourself, and you have realized it.

— *Your actions toward your mom hide your relationship with your son, because in entering in the relationship with your mom, you yourself are simultaneously mother for your son. When you change your relationship with your mom, your relationship with your son will change too, as the change will occur inside you.*

— The swinging process that occurs between the opposite sides of duality is very important and necessary. It allows you to accumulate the experience. You can become aware of this experience later when it is fully accumulated.

— *We can see that the weights of these opposite sides of the seesaw are equal. They are both strong and heavy. If that is not the case, we would not find it interesting and exciting to use this seesaw. It is very important to see that the opposite side of the seesaw is occupied by someone who is as strong and heavy as you are. Yes, you are strong in something, but he is strong in something else. Your strength, however, is equal. That's why you swing on this seesaw.*

— Those who swing on this seesaw have to see themselves as two sides of one coin.

I have activated the duality "rich—poor"

— *I have activated the duality "rich—poor". While I was rich, I used to create the conditions to experience poverty. As I receive the experience of poverty, I go to people who let me feel my poverty. I am tired of it.*

— Accept your poor part, and you will see how rich you are. Otherwise, your rich part cannot manifest itself. The rich part is only rich in comparison with a poor part.

— *One can even receive the money while being in different states. Everything depends on the state you happen to be in. If you happen to be in the state of a poor man, you will beg for the money as a beggar. This is just a state. Observe it. You can also receive the money while in a state of riches. How does a rich man receive his money? He calmly goes to the bank and takes out a loan, for example. He feels rich and conducts financial transactions easily. The bank lends him the money he asks for, and he uses it the way he thinks necessary. This state is opposite to the state of poverty.*

— You must feel your wealth. You can do it externally or internally, but only if you accept your poor part. Based on this, your inner rich part will feel its wealth. But by identifying with the poor part, you locked your rich part too.

— *I am experiencing a very unusual state during this seminar. Even though I am short of money, I don't feel the resistance of being here. Previously, I would have been anxiously running around trying to find money out of a state of fear. But now I am going to the seminar, knowing that people will help me to see this question from the inside. I don't even see it as a problem. I trust everyone here. This is the first time I have felt it. I feel grateful to you, Alexander Alexandrovich, for the opportunity you have created for me to experience this. This is a unique opportunity. I have felt our group like a creative laboratory where we experiment, receive certain results, and then use them. After I receive a certain experience here, I start to use it in other situations in my life. My mind was confused today. It was left without work. I don't have enough fear this time. This is a very unusual state. I saw every path my mind offered me, but I didn't follow them because all these paths were the paths of war. I see the assignment: I need money. How do I solve this problem? I decided not to think about it, to float along the river of life, and to release the situation. Once I let go of everything, I entered a state of de-identification with myself as a woman who needs money. I saw this woman from the side, and I experienced a desire to help her out of this difficult situation. I even found the whole situation funny. I decided to discuss this problem with one of my coworkers. I have passionately entered the role of my personage, feeling why I need this money. I just told her about this situation. I did not even ask her for money. Because of this conversation, my colleague started to feel what was going on, and she offered me the necessary sum of money.*

To discuss your problem instead of asking someone to solve it

— You have touched on some very important spot for her. That's why she reacted this way. This is the essence of the de-identified point of view on life. When you ask, demand, and insist on something, you activate the opposite side of duality, i.e. the resistance. When you simply discuss the state of your personage without having a direct desire to receive anything, a human being who listens to you develops a reciprocal feeling. I know that whatever happens will happen. I am not fixated on the goal, and I am not oppressing the one with whom I am discussing my state.

— *Exactly. I did not even think of asking to borrow money from her. I simply shared the story of my personage. The mind was not ready for such a turn of events. I was confused and did not know what to think of that.*

— Your mind got used to doing everything on its own, but you told someone about it. You declassified your mind. Your mind thought that this was the problem it should solve the usual way, i.e. to ask or beg for money. But you just told everything to your colleague.

— *The mind says, "It cannot be so simple." I got into a paradox. I was doing it for myself and not for myself at the same time.*

— *That's right. When you were discussing it with your coworker, you were discussing your situation in third person. You were neither rich nor poor.*

— When we are submerged in sleep, our life realizes the scripts of our personage. When we exit these scenarios, we find ourselves outside this mechanical game of conflict. We get into the state of "in this world, but not of this world". We enter the world of abundance. When you get there, the problems of your personage get solved in a very unusual way. These problems cannot be solved when you are in the world because every method that invites you to solve it is based on conflict and oppression. You will not find anything but the games of the personages in duality, manifested in the form of a fight, in the old matrix of consciousness. There is something else, but it happens to be outside the personages.

— *I did not want to ask her to give me the money. I have always tried to earn money.*

— To earn, by the way, is also to ask. When you apply for work, you fill out an application where the first words are "I ask to apply …" When you earn the money, you also ask. It just appears that you don't.

— *For me, there is no present, just past and future.*

— There is no present in the domain of the conditioned mind. It is constantly in the past, and it constantly drags the past into the future. But the new happens to be in the present. **Present is the moment when you can become aware of the past, and by changing your perception of the past you receive something different in the future.** The conditioned mind constantly drags the past into the future. As a result, we keep receiving the same thing all the time. The conditioned mind only sees its past in the future.

— *I activated the duality "like—don't like". I found a man who does not like me, and I want him to start liking me. I have not been very successful yet.*

— From the point of view of the conflict, the most interesting task is to get someone who does not like you to like you.

— *I see a fighter in me. I try to conquer him. I think I got into the duality "mother—child" again.*

— Mother and child are not a duality; those are roles. Personality performs different roles. For example, mother—child, man—woman, etc. but they are performed differently. We can ask the question, "Why are the same roles performed differently?" If this is a duality, it should be the same everywhere. The reason we observe that is that different dualities manifest themselves during role behavior. That makes this game very diverse. For example, good mother—bad mother. Even though it is not very clear sometimes what is "good" here and what is "bad". All these things require a detailed investigation. As the degree of our discernment is quite high now, we start to see the relativity of such notions as roles. A man and a woman do not represent a duality either. These are another pair of roles. Manifestations of dualities manifest themselves in the roles. As a result, performance of the roles varies.

— *There are many dualities in the role of a man and in the role of a woman. I don't understand all of them clearly.*

— That's true. As a result, when we use these words, we don't really understand what we mean.

— *We are getting deeper and deeper.*

— *I still think a man and a woman are a duality.*

— Yes, for example, they are opposite based on their bodies. Sexual attraction appears precisely because of this opposition between the physical bodies and presence of the sexual instinct. But the ways in which people perform different roles varies. Sometimes we see a man who manifests himself in the physical body of a woman. We frequently see the opposite scenario too—a woman manifested in the physical body of a man. We can frequently see sexual attraction between such people. Notions such as strong sex and weak sex are similarly unclear. Women who practice body building are stronger than most men. Sexual attraction as an instinct is downloaded for continuation of the species. This is a biological recreating program. A human being is constructed as a self-recreating creature. That's why the duality of masculine and feminine physical bodies was created, and sexual instinct was introduced. We can observe a similar program in the animal kingdom.

— *Yesterday we came to the conclusion that if it was not for the prohibition on sexuality, people would not give birth to children. They would just live for pleasure.*

When does a social animal find its life successful?

— What kind of pleasure are you talking about? This is a difficult question. Ask an average man what life is and what is its meaning. Most people will say, "The meaning of life is to give birth to children, to build a house, and to plant a tree." They see the meaning of life in the continuation of their ancestral tree.

The situation in which a man or a woman is infertile leads to a serious problem. So, it looks like a man is born to procreate. Some people will add that it is very important for them that their children have a good life. But what is "good"? No one can answer that question. The commonly accepted criteria are: more money, profession, family. As we can see, all these notions are based on the instinct to procreate inculcated into all human beings. This instinct is inculcated on the physiological level, but since a human being is a social animal, he dresses it up with different social illusions.

— *The role of the mother in which I found myself totally forbade me from expressing sexuality.*

— Your biological role has been completed.

— *I am Muslim. A program is being installed into Muslim women. According to Islam, a woman is forbidden from manifesting sexuality prior to getting married. A woman can only have sex if she is married. But as soon as I gave birth to my child, this rule was taken away from me—I am a mother now. Unmarried women find themselves in the worst situation. They are ostracized and "eat themselves from the inside."*

— Family is a cell of a society. As soon as the family breaks down, society starts to break down too. The ancestral matrix has very deep roots in Asiatic society. We do not see such a strong ancestral influence in western society. Family is a small cell of an ancestral clan. Its form must be preserved in order for society to function the way it presently functions.

— One cannot get out of this program.

A human being creates problems to receive experience

— You cannot jump out of certain specific programs of the old matrix without completely getting out of the matrix. You cannot make rest stops in the Process. People usually come here with a certain problem. They think they will get help in solving it. I show them that the problem exists only in their perception. The conditioned mind perceives life through certain notions. These notions are dual. Duality itself is a problem. Therefore, man's perception is always problematic and paradoxical. A man, the way he is now, will always have problems. A man is a collection of problems.

Reinforcement of the action of one side of a duality in respect to its opposite side is what is usually offered here as a solution to a problem. In this way, this side gets activated while the opposite side increases its resistance to such an action. However, the mind is not aware of this interconnectedness; it continues to "solve" the problem, i.e. to exacerbate it. We have discussed this already in connection with the process of the acquisition of personal experience.

A human being comes to this reality to receive the experience of divided perception, but being in a state of sleep, he doesn't understand that. The accumulation of this experience occurs through the activation of dualities in his personal structure with the following activation of them in the process of development of the personality. By living through and experiencing dualities inculcated in personality, a man calls them problems and tries to find methods to solve them. He thinks he must solve problems, but in reality, he just needs to receive a certain experience. It seems to him that problems are something external, and he tries to solve them as if they were something separate from himself. He thinks when he solves them he will be happy, but happiness doesn't come, even though he applies a lot of effort to solve these problems. Being in the divided perception, a man does not see that happiness is not a result of solving the problems he has but a consequence of understanding of who he really is.

In actuality, you can only solve a problem by getting outside the level of the dual perceptions that gave birth to it, i.e. by de-identifying with your personality. But to do that, you need to become aware of the inner mechanisms that give birth to these problems by seeing the mechanism of the action of dualities intrinsic to your personality. **In the end, you can exit this world and step into another world by remaining in this world and not reacting to it mechanically like a robot. You start to think paradoxically, i.e. to see the interplay of dualities in everything that happens in you and around you.**

Human language was created to describe technical devices, not the life of a Spirit

— It is difficult to express paradoxical thinking by using the currently available language system because it lacks the notions that describe non-dual states. All psychological notions build upon the contraposition of one side of a duality to its opposite side. Therefore, in order to express something that is outside duality, we have to use analogies and comparisons, which can be understood *only* by people who have already felt these states.

It is impossible to find words to describe something that exists in another world because that world is non-dual. The mechanism of human speech that is always based on certain notions reflects what exists in this world when it deals with technical terminology. For example, we take something we call a chair, and we say, "this is a chair." This will be right, as people call an object this symbol. We can take, for example, some mechanical parts of an automobile, such as a carburetor or a steering wheel. We will not have many problems here either. So, from the point of view of technical devices this language works pretty well. People who work with technology understand each other pretty well when they use this language. At least they can figure out what they are talking about. But when we start to touch upon things that create basic problems in life—freedom, truth, beauty, health, etc.—we stop understanding each other. At the same time, it appears to us as if we understand what these notions mean and that others should understand them too. If we were to take a carburetor, for example, many different versions of a carburetor exist today, and they can all be described and drawn pretty well. But what is beauty? What is freedom?

People understand these terms very differently. They put forward certain hypotheses regarding these notions, and then they change them. But no one can clearly define what they mean. Many people die for freedom, but what exactly is freedom? Freedom is usually seen as liberation from something, but in reality, freedom is needed not to liberate *from* something but to *do for* something. What do you need freedom for? Why do you think you don't have it now?

The language we use appeared as the result of our need to acquire a dual experience, and it reflects this dual experience. The experience a man acquires now is the experience of the conflict between opposites. When humanity becomes aware of this experience, a new language will appear. It will reflect the next quality of human experience, to which they will transfer with full understanding of their unity and interconnectedness with everything.

— *I frequently cannot find words to express what I experience.*

— Yes, this is a common situation. Moreover, whatever you don't have words for simply does not exist for the conditioned mind. Consider the scientific and technologic progress with which most people occupy themselves. Enormous amounts of money are spent on technology. Billions of dollars are spent on military alone. People are occupied with something that can be calculated and sorted in the name of some illusory, dual notions. But it is precisely such dual notions as freedom, independence, and protection of motherland that create the biggest problems that they attempt to solve by using weapons, for example.

Humanity is standing at the doorstep of understanding the mind

— How does human experience appear? How does an opportunity to investigate this experience appear? Animals also receive and accumulate certain experiences. However, they don't investigate it, even though it gets passed on genetically and fixed in certain models of behavior which contribute to survival of the species. Animal development occurs through the selection of the specimens better adapted to survive.

A human being consists of three parts: body, mind, and soul. A human being can also be seen from a point of another triad: body, soul, and spirit. A human being consists of three interwoven structures. Let's review the human body. It's a great apparatus which is currently programed to survive. Doctors and physiologists investigate intricate and well-coordinated mechanisms of the functioning of human body.

— *We, on the other hand, investigate the mind, its current abilities, and the possibility of exiting it.*

— Exactly. A human being is a social animal. Society, the way it is now, represents super-personality or super-ego. The processes that occurs in society reflects the processes that occur in personality. Neither society nor individual personalities are aware of these processes, since in order to become aware of them, one has to exit the borders of who one considers oneself to be. Therefore, enlightenment of a society is similar to enlightenment of an individual human being. But enlightenment of a society is only possible through enlightenment of the individual human beings who form it. Currently, there are about seven billion of them. Nature gave man a body. Society gave him personality. But neither nature nor society will offer to help him exit the borders of personality because they don't need that. This impulse comes from man's Spirit, i.e. from a part of a human being that happens to be in another world.

Every sensory organ of a human body perceives the physical body, and as a result, it has been investigated the best. The matter with which the human mind works is not perceived by physical vision, and as a result, we don't know much about the processing work of a human mind. What is thought, for example? How does it get born? A thought appears, evolves, and gets realized in certain material objects. But how does it appear? People don't know that yet. Scientists who investigate the mind are materially oriented, but unfortunately, it is impossible to come to know the subject we investigate from the physiological side.

— *Does psychoanalysis deal with it?*

— Psychoanalysis doesn't conduct physiological investigation. Psychoanalysis attempts to sort out how the mind operates. NLP and gestalt therapy pursue the same goal, but all these disciplines represent and investigate only fragments of our current notions of how the mind operates. They investigate certain particular aspects of the mind without investigating a human being as a whole. As a result, the set of notions they have developed, even though they are very interesting, is only one-sided.

In listening to what I say but not understanding what I transmit, you cannot catch the essence of the message

— What am I talking about? It is very important to understand what I pass on to you and what I do. That will allow you to better understand what you need to do. It is also very important to understand *how* I transmit what I transmit to you. Perhaps this is the main question, because by listening to what I say alone, without understanding what I transmit, you cannot grab the essence of it. That was quite a mouthful, but nevertheless. To simplify, I pass on awareness or an ability to self-investigate. This is the basic know how I have.

I share the results of my own self-investigation with you, but you cannot understand these results unless you have a passion for self-awareness. It must be the meaning of your life. You can only understand what I discuss as a self-investigator if you become one yourself. That's the only way. As I have said before, you should not simply believe me. You should conduct your own self-investigation and check everything I say yourself.

— *But it would be impossible for us to check everything you have done. Perhaps we can take your word for some of it?*

— No, that would impossible. If you do that, you would not understand that this is really the way it is because you did not experience it and did not become aware of it. In that case, you would only get what you get during your general education here, i.e. a certain knowledge that you accept to be true. In that case, you would start to believe in something that you have not personally experienced. You would get lost in the multiple illusions and become their slave. Knowledge related to the system of coordinates of the contemporary worldview is being transmitted as the Truth here. You accept it and start to see the world according to it while not even questioning its potential relativity.

I am not transmitting the Truth here. Moreover, I explain that you are the only one who can discover it inside yourself, and the process of this discovery is very interesting. I pass on to you an opportunity to conduct self-investigation. If you have an impulse for self-investigation, you will start to accept and understand it only because you start to do it yourself. If you don't do it on your own, it doesn't exist for you. I teach you the basic principles of how to conduct the correct self-investigation, and during this Process we share our experiences and the results we receive. But for someone who doesn't have an impulse for this work, those are just empty words.

— *When I talk to my friends and relatives about what we do here, most of them are not interested in it at all.*

Self-investigation is investigation of the essence of the experiences we are currently in

— Let's take a closer look at the self-investigation process. It never stops. It constantly changes. It leads us to understand who we are at this moment and where we are moving toward. Self-investigation uncovers the quality of the experience we are currently in. Our Process is a constant movement toward a better understanding of ourselves and of this reality.

— *If we have chosen to live in this dual world, we should investigate the mechanisms on which it operates, and at the end we see what we acquire and accumulate while living here.*

— Let's return to the question of what self-investigation is and where does the impulse to conduct it is come from. Why do some people have it while others don't? Most people never experience this impulse. It comes from the Spirit through the emotional center. This is the direct channel of connection with the Soul and the Spirit, which happens to not be in this world.

The conditioned mind and the physical body are in this world. When we transfer to another world, we leave our physical body here, but we take the experience we accumulate here with us. The body and the mind are one organism that can only be investigated by something that is outside of both the body and the mind. If we take science, for example, it comes from the mind and is conducted by the mind, i.e. it's the mind that investigates its own birth. But being inside itself, it cannot see itself holistically.

The impulse of self-investigation comes from something that is outside the mind. While in the three being structures made out of the body, mind, and soul, we live a divided life. Every one of the three composite elements that we can call "I" has its own aims, which are quite often mutually exclusive. Living in such a strange way, we don't know about that, and as a result get surprised by the dramatic situations in which we find ourselves, as well as the states we experience. We get irritated by them, and we start to blame and condemn ourselves or others.

— *Life frequently signals us ahead of time, but we often don't see these signals. Let's return to the situation of my wallet being picked from my purse on the bus. The thought of changing that old wallet has been popping into my head over the last few months, but I didn't hear myself. In the end, I attracted a thief who stole it from me. That was my way to let go of the old wallet. This scene could have been played differently, but I didn't hear my inner voice.*

— Our personality lives based on the scenario created by two opposite directors who express two opposite sides of the dualities it contains. But the sleeping personality is only conscious of one of them. As a result, whatever the second, subconscious director does is considered by it to be a failure and a shock. To become whole is to become aware of the two opposite directors in you as one whole and to clearly see that they both need each other. This is a holistic view of your personality.

You cannot define the Soul. You can only experience it.

— You will not be able to understand the nature of the Soul based on mental notions alone. There are many definitions of a Soul, but you will not come to know your Soul even if you come to know all of them. You cannot define what a Soul is, but you can experience it. To be constantly aware of your personality and of your physical body is to experience yourself as a Soul. Self-investigation will lead you to become aware of yourself as a wholesome three-body essence.

When you become aware of your three-body essence, you will become fully aware of your intention and will be capable of creating according to this intention. Until you are in a separated, fragmented state, you will continue to fight yourself. You are both the fighter and the one who is being fought. Not being fully aware of the scriptwriter and the directors of our show, we continue to be unhappy with the show that is being played on the playground of our life.

The script writer of this show is your Soul. Two directors are our dual mind. The actor is our physical body. The show of our life in dual reality is staged by two twin-directors. The astrological twin sign is a good symbol for them. Two human beings are looking in opposite directions while standing back to back. They don't see each other, but they feel each other very well. One of them creates "I want that" while the other creates "I don't want that" or "I want the opposite of that". During every minute of his life, man's conditioned mind is conscious of the desires of one director only, and it realizes it while overcoming the resistance created by the opposite director, the director it is not even conscious of.

At the same time, the scriptwriter writes the script for both directors, and they both direct this show having equal rights. They act simultaneously, but they act in opposite directions, as two sides of a pair of scissors. But I want to repeat that the conditioned mind only identifies itself with one of the directors. It doesn't accept the creativity of the other director. It perceives him as bad and unnecessary, i.e. as something he doesn't expect from life.

— *The situation with Olga's wallet being stolen is very characteristic. She had an impulse, "I want to change this wallet." She didn't react to it. She didn't realize it. So, another director created a small robbery.*

— Olga didn't accept this impulse because she identified herself with the part that did not want to part with this wallet. Her director said, "This is our wallet. We are not going to give it to anyone." The other director said, "No. It's time to part with it," and it created the scene on the bus. But this scene was appraised from the position of the other, conscious director who didn't want to part with the wallet. When the director that didn't want to part with the wallet sees a thief pick up the wallet, he gets angry and unhappy.

As you can see, both directors have equal rights in staging the show of your life. They realize the opposite tendencies of dualities present in your personality. One is black, the other is white. One is yin, the other—yang.

— *You have to listen to yourself very carefully. When you feel the impulse to change something, your wallet for example, you must do it. In this case, you don't have to lose the money and experience unnecessary losses. If you feel the impulse— do it.*

— The loss of a wallet represents a certain physical action that leads to a certain result, and not only physical. Everything has been accounted for by the scriptwriter, but one of your directors cannot understand what's going on because the script of your life is being written in duality, paradox, and opposition. The theft of a wallet is not just a loss of money; it's an action that can lead to a change in your perception of yourself or to habitual disappointment, irritation, condemnation, and self-pity.

— *It's quite possible that this theft will be followed by some inner changes in me.*

— This is not simple, but it is possible. Let me use my own example. During the last seminar in Ekaterinburg, I encountered a woman who offered me a massage. I agreed. After this massage, I developed furuncles on my back. Reviewing this situation on the level "disease—health", we can see that I got sick. So, I invited her into my life in order for her to play out a certain role which led me to experience a serious disease. This vision of the scene of the show of my life forced me to become aware of the duality that was activated by me. The results of seeing this duality are many, and it is impossible to become aware of all of them immediately. I become slowly aware of them as I experience the activated duality.

— *I feel that by parting with this wallet I have also parted with poverty. It was bought when I was very poor.*

— What can we do while being asleep? To say that we can become totally aware of everything that the scriptwriter of our dream creates means to get out of this dream, i.e. to finish this investigation. Therefore, we agree with the fact that we cannot yet understand everything the scriptwriter does, but we can continue to investigate it.

— *That's very interesting.*

— Yes, but when we resist the script, we suffer. That's what most people do. On the other hand, we can stop resisting and start to become aware of it, understanding that everything that happens to us, from trivial to important things, happens based on a well-determined plan of the show of our life, the show that we need to experience and to become aware of.

Your Soul directs your show, but do you hear what it says?

— You can perform it while not accepting so-called negative. That's what most people do. As a result, they play out drama and tragedy.

What does it mean to be a good actor? A good actor can play the script of his show correctly and beautifully. **The impulse that comes from a Soul is perceived by the heart. This is the channel through which we intuitively feel the next act of our show. We feel it, and we perform it.** The life of a sleeping man is not based on intuition; it is lived according to the conditioned mind. He is tuned in to react and analyze. This is something an actor does who does not feel what the scriptwriter needs.

— *He usually plays very badly.*

— He plays the way he is used to: with suffering, pain, condemnation, and guilt.

— *He sometimes plays this role masterfully.*

— A man who is torn away from and not aware of his Soul plays his show like a martyr, suffering. He cannot transform it because there is no contact between the actor and the screenwriter. The screenwriter downloads the script into the mind by forming two twin-directors in it. By being unaware of the duality of your directors, you will only play drama; you will mechanically fight for the title of the exclusively-dramatic actor. Then you will die just to be reborn again in order to play another dramatic role, the mechanism of which will be analogous. This situation will continue until you start to become aware of the duality of your perception. Being a self-investigator requires an ability to change the plan of the script of your life by becoming aware of the dual mechanism of your personality. This ability can only be acquired through self-investigation.

— *A few years ago, I read the memoirs of great actors. They spoke about the way they played their roles. All of them talked about feeling the role and about one's need to live it through. Sometimes they would identify with a certain role so strongly that they would have trouble getting out of it. Sometimes they would realize the scripts of their personages in their own life.*

— We know of many instances where actors could not get de-identified with their role. The scripts of the old matrix may vary, but they are identical in their essence. One can only exit out of them by becoming aware of the mechanisms by which all the scripts of the old matrix of consciousness get realized. Those are the mechanism of the functioning of personal dualities.

As human creatures who happen to be in the old matrix, we mechanically play out its dual scripts, the essence of which is fear and suffering. This is the dream in which we live. Many different scripts are being played out here, but all of them represent just one variation of one theme, which consists of a conflict between one part of false personality and the other part of it.

What do we do with the help of self-investigation? We reach the essence of all the scripts of the old matrix. We see that all these scripts on the level of a human being, group of people, nation, country, and civilization vary somewhat, but in essence, they are all identical in their basic manifestations, i.e. in the mechanisms of their functioning. Country is a big ego. Family is a smaller ego. Human being is a little ego. We see that every ego acts in accordance to a certain law. We can see why and how different scripts are created on the level of personality, family, corporation, or country because all of them repeat themselves in this sense.

Find dependency in independence

— Let's take the duality "dependence—independence". It is interesting because a human being experiences many difficulties in interacting with other people. We are incapable of not interacting as

92

it is precisely through our interactions with other people that we come to know who we are. If we don't define ourselves by creating different relationships, we would not know who we are. It is precisely in our relationships with other people that what we call dependency develops. It gives birth to its opposite side—independence.

For example, a woman who receives money from a man becomes dependent on him. The appearance of this duality is connected with the fear for her future, where he may not give her the money. This fear starts to stimulate the other side, and she says that she doesn't want to be dependent on him—she wants to be independent. How can she get this independence? For example, she can go to work and start to earn money on her own. But in that case, she will become dependent on this work. After working for some time, she may start to get irritated, for example on account on her dependency on a small salary or dumb supervisor. She may start to search for new employment where she will be paid more. But this is another dependency. Therefore, in fighting for independence, she will always be in touch with dependence.

— *One way or another, she will always be dependent on something.*

— Exactly. We have examined the case scenarios connected to money, but we can see it everywhere. For example, when I say I love you, I start to see my dependence on you. In this case, it's better for me not to love you. That will offer me independence. At the core of interaction of the polar sides of duality always lies fear. One side is always afraid of its opposite side and, as a result, fights against it. This fear is chronic, but as the conditioned mind explains it based on its one-sided perception, it leads to the condemnation of the external cause of this fear. Explaining the reasons behind fear by these external factors forces the personage to fight the factors. Such conflict, however, only exacerbates fear.

As we can see, this situation is a dead-end. We cannot exit the fear that appears as a result of the fight between two opposite sides of duality while we are identified with a duality. You can now clearly see the illusory nature of the presupposition that we can simply move from dependence to independence.

— *The reacher the man is, the higher the level of his fear.*

— The healthier the man is, the higher the level of his fear of getting sick. The higher the man's status, the higher the level his fear of losing it. The more you have of something that you want to hold on to, the more fear you have of losing it, and the stronger is the swing of this duality. That's exactly where the mind gets lost: by defining the problem, it starts to search for the solution. But it doesn't disappear. What's even more interesting is that it cannot disappear. What exactly do you consider yourself to be dependent on?

— *I am dependent on people's opinions of me. I want to be independent of them.*

— How can you get rid of this dependency?

— *I attract other people to my side and counter both these two sides. For example, if I am told I am a bad specialist, I will bring five people who will say the opposite.*

— Do you think you can get rid of your dependency on other people's opinions this way? Initially, you were dependent on the opinion of one man. Then, you brought five more men, whose opinions you also depend on, in order to show your independence from the opinion of the first man. Look, by fighting for independence from someone's opinion, you become dependent on somebody else's opinion. The example you have brought up clearly demonstrates that dependence and independence are two sides of one coin.

In fighting for independence, you become even more dependent. You remain dependent, and the fear persists because these five can declare you to be a bad specialist tomorrow. You can bring hundreds of people, but you will not get rid of this dependency, because you are using it in your fight for independence. You are dependent on the opinions of other people. You just manipulate the opinion of one of them in relation to the other five. That's what politicians do.

Politics represents a very strong dependency on the opinions of others. That's what it is built upon. Every propaganda campaign builds on the ability of a party leader to form a positive opinion toward himself and his party. Who is he, in reality? Who knows? Every contemporary politician has an image-making team.

Image is a form of illusion that overemphasizes the positively perceived personality traits of a candidate. Take Yeltsin, for example. He is very slow. Therefore, it is necessary to show him being fast, and he is shown playing tennis on TV. His image-makers show the side of him that is directly opposite to the side with which he is identified as a personality. He is shown as fast-acting. This image is introduced and inculcated into the minds of voters.

Which one of you knows Yeltsin? The average voter doesn't know him and will never know him. The average voter is offered a certain positively-colored image. As a result, politics always represents dependency on the opinion of the majority, at least in so-called democratic countries. We can see how similar the behavior of an average personality and the personality of a government official creating government policy is. The only difference is that a politician creates illusions by using specialists who knows how to do it professionally.

Where does the exit out of dependency lead?

— We have discussed that "dependency—independency" is one duality. I asked you how you propose to get out of dependency. You have answered my question. But as we can see now, by doing what you have proposed to do, you maintain your dependency. Moreover, you exacerbate it. By fighting for independence, you use dependence.

It appears to you that you are getting rid of it, but in reality, you exacerbate it even more. That's what we do all the time.

On what are people dependent? Let's work with some real life examples. I repeat that the life of a human being represents a dependency on everything with which he connects. Let's list these dependencies.

— *A man depends on his boss, the weather, attention, money, feelings, mood, the place he lives, the food he eats, his children, status, the time of the year, the city he lives in, the country he lives in, etc.*

— Everything that is connected with any kind of interaction—with a situation, a thing, a human being—can turn into dependency. Everything turns into dependency. You cannot solve a problem by fighting dependency. That only exacerbates it. Do you understand that?

I will ask you to review what you depend on and what you do by fighting for your so-called independence based on the examples from your own life. Any interaction of people is always "dependence—independence" from the point of view of the conditioned mind. Love is also "dependence—independence". We call the force that attracts one human being to another human being love. But from the point of view of the mind, it is called "dependence—independence", and in the end, it leads to conflict.

— *Now I can clearly see my dependence on my partner, and at the same time, I can see that my girlfriend, who doesn't have a partner, is similarly dependent on the absence of a partner.*

— I will ask you to pick an important person in your life and to investigate whether you are dependent on him or her or independent from them. You will feel dependency on every human being who is important for you. For example, you are independent from a passerby you happen to bump into on the street. But what if we were to discuss a human being who is close to you and with whom you interact all the time? You are dependent on him. Eventually, this dependency starts to bother you, and you develop a desire to free yourself of it.

— *Does it have to bother me?*

— If you take a close look at your relationships with the people who are close to you, you will see that you feel dependent on them. You can hate a man or love him, but the essence is the same, because both relationships represent dependency. You hate, and you depend on this state. You love, and you also feel dependence. Going deeper, you will see that the basic script of the game "dependence—independence" was acquired during your relationship with your parents. Later, it was realized in your relationships with the people who are close to you.

— *Yes. In my case, my dependency on the image of my mother is being realized now in my relationship with my son. I used to be afraid of what my mother would say about me. Now I am afraid what he is going to say about me. The matrix itself appeared because of my interaction with my mother.*

— Your mother and father may have passed by now, but the matrix of perception inculcated by them remains, and it recreates itself in your relationships with other people. Let's look at your dependency on your father and mother, and at the methods you use to try and exit it. This is characteristic for all teenagers. They feel dependency on their parents and try to free themselves from it by using different methods. This leads to a state of conflict in the duality, which they recreate later in their adult life.

The fight for independence is fought to change the rules

— A child feels a strong dependency on his parents. He starts to protest and says, "I am independent! I am on my own!" He asserts that one way or another. It is impossible for him not to assert that, as otherwise his personality will not be formed. A child starts to break the rules that were set by those he depends on and introduces his own rules. So, independency is the introduction of one's own rules. But later on, you will be very irritated by the kids who do the same, i.e. you will create the same model of behavior for them. You will do what your parents have done in creating certain rules for you, while your own kids will try to break these rules. You must see this continuity. This is the eternal conflict of parents and children.

The fight in the sphere of duality "dependence—independence" is one of the most important dualities for a human being, which cannot be solved by using a traditional approach. The only thing this approach can do is to constantly recreate the same dual matrix accompanied by the screams of the fight for independence. That's exactly what your children will do fifteen years down the road. And their children will do the same.

Take a close look at your "dependence—independence" in relationship with your parents. What did it consist of? Look at how you started to fight for your independence. What did you do? Review this duality in detail and you will see the reasons why your children do what they do in respect to you.

— *I can clearly see that my daughter repeats everything I did, but her way of doing it is harsher than mine. I ran away from parents by getting married. She did not get married. She just gave birth to a child. I can clearly see that, but how can I get out of it?*

— You move too fast. You don't see it clearly yet. If you were to see it clearly, you would not ask what to do about it. "I see" — means "I got out". If you say that you see, but you have not exited the situation, you don't see it holistically. If I see, I am out. If I am not out, I don't see.

— *My parents used to give me a lot of freedom. They were very busy. They used to go to work where we were still asleep, and by the time they would come home we would be in bed already. I have been dependent on my parents' attention. They tried to give it to us kids. For example, every Sunday we would have breakfast together and have a picnic in the afternoon. Yet, I didn't have enough parental. As a result, I moved to another town after high school, even though I could have stayed in my native city.*

— What exactly do you see as dependency? Is it too little or too much attention? Attention is an interesting thing. For example, someone came and spat at you. This is attention. One can easily get it by insulting someone.

Someone caressed you. It's attention. Someone hit you. It's attention. Someone shot at you—it is also attention. To kill a man is to manifest a high degree of interest toward him. You were dependent on what kind of attention?

— *I was dependent on the positive appraisal by my parents and their positive communication with me. I was dependent on my being different than my siblings. When coming home for summer break, I felt this attention. My parents made me feel special.*

Every child depends on his parents. That's what leads him to rebel.

— A child depends on his parents in terms of food, clothing, and housing. Many parents are ready to provide for their children, but only on the condition that they will absorb their program, i.e. their notions of what is good and what is bad. Parents do not just feed their children. They inculcate his or her personality with their notions of what is right and what is wrong, what is good and what is bad. Such a dependency of a child on his parents leads to conflict between them.

During adolescence, children start to revolt. They start to take care of themselves as independent personalities, and to declare who they are. This declaration manifests itself through the fight for independence, i.e. by asserting their beliefs and convictions. The transition period is the age of their fight for independence, i.e. the age when newly a budding and forming personality asserts itself. Personality does this by negating the rules inculcated by parents, at least some of these rules. That's how parents download the matrix of dualities into the personality of a child. Later, their child reinforces it by fighting them.

— I used to fight the image of a proper girl as a teenager. I would wear pants, run around with boys, and ride a motorcycle. In the end, I turned into a man in a woman's body. This was very uncomfortable.

— Your independence was based on your dependence on the image of a proper girl. In trying to overcome this dependence, you moved to the image of a boy.

— Yes. Later on, feeling financial dependence, I started to support myself as a truly independent man. I was studying nursing during by day and working as a paramedic at night.

— Independence is a proclamation and assertion of one's own personality. In your case, its basic aspects are: "I can act like a boy. I can be financially independent. I can live on my own." Personality manifests itself in its fight for independence from what it considers itself to be dependent on. We call it activation of duality.

Different personalities view different things as dependencies. Children brought up in one family may fight for different things because they form different personal structures. You should understand on what your personality was formed. The development of personality occurs through assertion of independence, which is based on seeing something as dependence. If you didn't assert your independence, you did not form your personality, because personality gets strengthened only in the fight between opposites. Look at your life and sort out on which dualities and what assertion of the sides of these dualities your personality was formed.

— I asserted my personality by living at home and getting married. My parents, especially my father, kept me in fear and limitations. When I got married,

I started to assert myself as a personality in front of my husband. In the end, I ran away from him too.

— You assert your personality by running away. This is one of the ways personality asserts itself.

— *Yes, instead of being with people like you, I would rather be on my own.*

— So, your experience of interacting with people will be painful. Even if you go for it, you will eventually wind up on your own. As we can see, personality forms in the fight for independence, while independence is the opposite side of the dependency in which a child happens to be. The question a child faces is what to consider a dependency. By defining something as a dependency, a child will fight tooth and nail to acquire what is opposite to it, i.e. independence. That's how a child forms his personality. When personality is formed, a child recreates and reinforces it.

A human being tries all his life to get out of the dualities that form his personality. This is a vicious circle. This paradoxical mechanism works like a Perpetua mobile. One can only get out of it by becoming aware of it. Otherwise, your script will be transferred to your children, who will recreate it and pass it on to their children. This is what ancestral karma is about. That's why it is so difficult to accept one's parents as the personality of a child forms in opposition to the qualities of its parents. Meanwhile, the dualities present in the personalities of parents and their children are identical. In this way, we are connected to them at all times by the law of karma, irrespective of whether they are dead or alive.

To accept your parents, you must accept yourself holistically, i.e. you have to accept both the positive and negative sides of your personality. But how can you accept yourself holistically if your personality builds on its independence from the negative? There is only one exit out of this paradoxical circle: to see dependence and independence as two sides of one coin. This is the only way to exit the dualities of your personality. Otherwise, your personal program works silently.

— *It is very hard to get out of program. It is like a tram that is running down well-known tracks.*

— No one said that it will be easy.

— *One can fear dependency. When one gets out of fear, the state of dependency disappears. One can start to interact instead.*

— Yes, the conflict between dependence and independence is based on fear. Dependence is based on the fear that I will not get what I think I want, while independence is based on the fear that I will become dependent on it. The entire matrix of duality is based on fear. Are you ready to start to move out of the paradox of duality, i.e. out of fear?

Familial matrix of fears is transmitted to us by our parents

— *I observed myself today. I observed the parts of me that create. I was late to the seminar, even though I did everything I could to be here on time. I somehow wound up getting on a bus that took me in the opposite direction. When I got out of it, I realized I was late. I asked myself, "What's going on?" and I immediately saw a very familiar part of me. This part doesn't need anything. It doesn't want any changes. It would lie in front of the TV drinking tea all day long instead of investigating the mind. Moreover, this investigation is death to it. I have met with the creativity of this part a few times already. I could see this part only through its creation.*

— **Seeing is action: you can change what you see.** We create everything we are afraid of in our lives. I invite you to review the models of your parents' lives. Which one of these two matrixes did you take to form the conscious part of your personality, and which one of them formed your subconscious part? What were your parents afraid of? Their fears were transmitted to you. These fears got fixed in your personality. They realize themselves mechanically now.

— *My mom was afraid of my dad. This fear was transmitted to me. I am afraid of men too. As a child, I was afraid of my dad. Later on, I was afraid of my brother, husband, and boss. I grew up, but this fear is still in me. Yesterday, when my brother got home, I felt something new. I usually feel fear when I see him. It usually expresses itself in physical discomfort. I get anxious. My brother has been living with us for the last twelve months. I lived in this state for the whole year. I observed my fear of him all this time. For the first time, I felt calm yesterday when my brother came. I observed this calmness. My mind started to fidget. I kept observing. I was not in fear. I was observing. That was a totally different state. Eventually, we had a difficult conversation, but I did not feel fear throughout it. I felt interest. We could have a long and successful conversation. This was very unusual not only for us but for the whole family, which gathered around us. This was two actors in a show. We were surrounded by silent spectators, but their eyes betrayed their interest. I felt excited. I was playing my role fearlessly. I was surprised with myself and happy that I could carry out this role in such calm way, even though the mind tried to suck me back into my usual, habitual state. I was aware of my mind. I was outside of it, in the observer. When the conversation ended, his eyes were warm; they expressed gratitude. I was experiencing the same feelings. I had a feeling that I had passed a very important test that dealt with the fear of physical oppression by men. I had passed through many stages with my brother during this year. We screamed and fought, but in the end we got to this heart-to-heart conversation. I have never experienced anything like that. I was filled with joy.*

— You have passed the exam on how to follow your intention and how to feel the vibrations of love. You have participated in the Process for three years. It is not easy to enter these vibrations, but it is even more difficult to maintain them inside yourself, to live in them while surrounded by the lower vibrations related to father, brother, husband, physical abuse, and alcoholism. You could maintain the vibration of love. Moreover, you have allowed your brother to feel it—his eyes got warmer. He tried many methods to bring you back to the vibration of fear: he drank alcohol, screamed at you, and fought you. But you kept your intention. What kind of an intention is it? Why is it so powerful? The mind cannot understand it. Only the heart can feel it.

— *My intention led me like a good compass. I walked based on feelings alone.*

— The way of the heart goes through feelings. For example, an arm of the compass points north. When you get to the North Pole, you will not see anything there. The sign that specifies that this is the extreme point was placed there by people who used very sensitive instruments. One should be very sensitive enough to feel that. That's what happened between you and your brother. It was very difficult for you to open his feeling center. You had to descend to the very deepest level of fear.

— *I saw my dad's program of oppression in me; it started to work in relationship to my daughter. She started to come home late, and I got very nervous about it. I started to scream at her, and I felt a desire to spank her a couple times. But then I saw that I was doing to her exactly what my dad did to me. He was a despot. He insisted we follow every rule of his. I observed myself. Based on his program, I had to insist my kids do the same. I started to do that already; the program got turned on automatically. When I saw it, I decided to change it. Two days after the fight, I got my daughter to sit down for a cup of tea with me, and we had a conversation. I didn't blame or threaten her. I made sure there was no fear there. I felt relieved and satisfied. I felt this method was working. Thank you!*

— I congratulate you. What you did was a very difficult thing to do. The programs we are dealing with are very harsh. They are strongly ingrained in us and work automatically. **We can only change them by becoming aware of them.** This is not a fast process. We must observe and see fear in detail. Then, we must investigate it. No one can do this for us.

— This is a very intricate process. I was pulling on the "threads" that lead to my parents and grandparents every day. I meditated daily, and one day it started to manifest itself in the physical world. Every familial program of fear and oppression got activated in me before this seminar. I accepted it and started to see what was happening to me from the point of view of observing the program while simultaneously submerging into it. I was diving deep, but I couldn't do anything about this program. I was simply thrown from one side of duality to another. One cannot exit this program without the help of awareness. One just repeats it mechanically.

Why don't we study self-investigation in middle school?

— We are talking about family now. Look at a nation now. It's a big family. Every nation has its own set of problems, its own peculiarities. They can only be solved through real changes in a big number of people. A nation should feel itself as a big family. It should rid itself from the karmic heritage of old programs.

— This would have happened much faster if self-investigation was taught in middle school.

— Parents would not allow their kids to know more about themselves than they know themselves. They will allow it in terms of many different subjects but not in terms of life. The level of the consciousness of parents should be high enough for them to be higher than their own ego. Only in that case will kids study self-investigation in schools.

— Parents constantly talk to their kids about how tough life treats them.

— Parents say, "You don't understand me" and proceed to create a script of life for their children. The child lives through it and says, "Yes, I feel as bad as you did. I understand you now".

— Some parents do it diferently. They try to protect their kids from everything, and then they get surprised: "Why is he so irresponsible?"

— Children will not understand it until their parents do. Perhaps kids will study self-investigation as a main subject in school one day once people become aware of its necessity and importance. A child's personality has not been formed yet, and therefore, he cannot perceive many things the understanding of which requires him to have a more extensive life experience. The way a child's personality will be formed depends on adults. Kids will resemble their parents. It is possible to provide this type of education in specialized schools. To pass along principles of self-investigation, we will need teachers to teach it and parents to send their kids to such schools with a full understanding of why they do that.

— *You are talking about schools of the future.*

— *Schools, the way they exist at the present time, simply destroy kids' creative abilities. I teach middle school, and I sometime give kids assignments connected to creativity. They have a difficult time grasping what is asked of them. Moreover, most of them don't even want to understand what I ask them to do.*

— It is not easy to get out of the old matrix of consciousness, but it's much more difficult to live in it.

CHAPTER 4

THE ILLUSIONS—INHERITANCE THAT PARENTS PASS ON TO THEIR CHILDREN

•◆•◆•◆•◆•◆•◆•◆•◆•◆•◆•◆•◆•◆•◆•◆•◆•◆•◆•

Faith that is based on fear leads to the materialization of fear

— I invite you to discuss familial fears. How do we pass them on from generation to generation? What were your parents afraid of? How do you materialize these fears in your life? Let's investigate our parents as our mirrors and look at which parts of ourselves they reflect back to us. One peculiar feature of a human being consists of his ability to see himself in a mirror. Most animals, when in front of the mirror, don't understand that they see themselves. A man, on the other hand, understands that he sees himself when he stands in front of a mirror. But in the physical mirror he only sees his physical body. We are studying the old psychological matrix of consciousness. To do that, we need special mirrors. I ask you to use your parents as mirrors. You have not looked at them this way before. You used to see them only mechanically. I invite you to see a new vision. I also invite you to become aware of what you see.

— *I was very afraid of Dad's dying.*

— Who gave you this fear?

— *I took it from Mom. She was much younger than Dad. All her life, she was afraid he would die before her. This fear was realized in the end. She lives by herself now. He has been dead for many years now.*

— Real is what you believe to be real. The notion of one or another type of fear as being real, death of a father for example, is introduced into a child by different people. You took this fear in. It took a certain form. You started to believe in the reality of this fear, and it materialized. Can you see this fear as something that was passed on to you, something that should not necessarily be implemented by you, unless you invest your own belief in it? Our beliefs create everything. You started to believe in the reality of fear, and it materialized itself. Can you see this fear as something that was passed on to you? Can you see that you don't have to fulfill it unless you invest your own beliefs in it? As I have said already, our beliefs create everything. As fear rules here, our beliefs come out of fear, i.e. I believe in something I fear, and I materialize it. I find an actor who believes my fears, and both of us star in a thriller.

— *But my dad really did pass away.*

— That's right. This fear was very strong, and you have realized his death out of this fear. But you don't have to take it all the way to the level of realization. You can see it earlier and stop it.

— *I have a fear of ruining my relationships with the people around me. I see how I create this fear. When I was young, I was afraid to ruin my relationship with my mom. To avoid this danger, I forbade myself to perceive her to be good. I only saw her as a bad mother. This was very convenient for me.*

— Did you do it yourself?

— *Yes, I did it myself. I confess that.*

— Your example is very characteristic of this reality. It is much more convenient to blame other people, including our parents, for deteriorated relationships.

— *No, I don't want to blame anyone. This was convenient for me. My mom would come home in different moods all the time. I was a sensitive child, and I suffered because of it. So, in order to not be afraid of her all the time, I created a bad image of her in my head.*

— Yes, then everything is normal; your expectations are fulfilled.

— *Even if she is good to me today, I know that she is really bad. This knowledge affects every aspect of my relationships. For example, this image has been superimposed on my relationship with my husband. Dad was the only one who I perceived to be good. I forbade him to be bad. That's how I started to control my parents. I found myself dependent on what I had created.*

— You tried to get out of dependency, but as it turned out, you became even more dependent. Look at how fear takes certain concrete forms in the life of a human being. I can't just be afraid. I should be afraid of something. This "something" starts to materialize. It takes a certain scripted role that starts to develop in the life of a human being. One's life can contain many such lines.

Fear should be objectified and then realized. We realize it by screaming and crying. That's exactly how we do it when we realize our creativity through fear. But we can also realize it through Unconditional Love. However, this is a totally different system of coordinates. But unless you get out of fear, you cannot get into this different system. You can get out of fear only by seeing the mechanisms on which fear works in detail, i.e. the mechanisms of the work of duality. You will see that everything you create in your life comes out of a duality that gives birth to fear. Therefore, you need to open these dualities and get out of them.

We inherit our parents' fears

— *When I spoke to Mom about our family, she told me about Dad's desire to have many kids. There are three of us, but he wanted more. Mom had many abortions out of fear that they would not be able to support all of us. I have started to realize the same fear for survival in my life. I would not allow myself to have a child out of fear that I would not be able to provide for him.*

— *I have developed my mom's fear of her father betraying her. I have realized this fear in my life. Both of my husbands were unfaithful to me.*

— You say "fear of betrayal," but I believe that you desire to be betrayed. We create the situation of betrayal to get pluses out of it later. For example, you can blame the guy who betrayed you: "Look at you. I was faithful to you, but you…"

109

— That's right. Dad has always felt guilty around Mom.

— It is easy to manipulate someone who feels guilty. Try to see that your mom was interested in this betrayal because she could manipulate him by using the feeling of guilt afterwards.

— Mom saved his life during the war. I thought her fear of losing him started there.

— The fear of loss through death is one thing, but he can, for example, leave for another woman.

— When a woman starts to control her man too harshly, he leaves. He will either find another woman or die. One way or another, he will realize this fear.

— Yes. We have seen many such cases.

— That's what happened. Dad died, and Mom said, "I thought I loved him, but deep down I hated him." She fully realized her fear.

— She didn't have a choice. We create our lives, but we don't understand what we create. By seeing other women, your father was trying to prolong his life, so to speak. If he didn't play around on the side, he would have been physically destroyed. Death would be the next step for him. His move to another woman was a gentler exit. I have seen many such situations in families with many children, where wives were very fearful of their husbands leaving for another woman, and they suddenly died.

— Woman creates a certain emotional state, and man realizes it.

— Exactly. Woman creates a certain emotional state, and man realizes it.

— I am afraid of making people upset.

— You constantly realize your fear of being upset by someone. That's where your fear of upsetting others comes from. You must make some people upset to feel both sides. People constantly upset you. You invent different methods to prevent yourself from getting upset, but you preserve this fear of yours. When we finally find duality, we see that fear is behind it. If we verbalize this fear, we can see it and become aware of it. You are afraid of getting other people

110

upset. Nevertheless, you upset people, but you don't see it. Where does all of this come from? It comes out of your fears, which are framed in certain notions.

You don't see these fears right away. They manifest themselves as fragments, but you don't have any instructions on what to do with them. Our Process is like a puzzle. We collect ourselves piece by piece. But to do that, you need to know the picture that you intend to gather together. I keep reminding you about this picture. If you try to invent this picture, based on illusory fantasies, you will gather together a false picture. This false picture will not work.

— *I sometimes don't know what to do with it.*

Look for duality everywhere and in everything!

— Yes. Every part of the personality looks like a fragment in the inner world, yet each fragment wants to pretend that it is whole. The basic topic we discuss is duality. You must always search for duality. When you start to see duality, you start to see your inner fragments. If you don't see duality, you don't know what to look for and what to connect. The essence of self-investigation is to collect yourself in one holistic picture, which we collect from our own fragments.

— *One can see the picture but be unable to assemble it.*

— In that case, it will remain abstract and unrealized.

— *I asked you a question yesterday: "Can I trust your words?" I answered my own question today. The knowledge you carry is priceless, but only my own experience turns this knowledge into awareness.*

— Exactly. Knowledge, feelings, and experience are necessary for a holistic understanding of yourself. One component alone will not lead you anywhere. Many people come here asking to be allowed just to listen to what I say. I tell them it's pointless; it will not do them any good.

Someone comes and starts to experience the usual state that is habitual for him. He doesn't hear what we discuss at the level of new knowledge. He sees it superficially, based on the habitual scheme "yes—no", "agree—disagree". You will not be able to assemble a whole picture of yourself this way.

You can compile your fragments in one whole only if you have a correct picture of what you need to compile in front of your eyes. Actually, you cannot see this picture. You can only feel that you are moving in the right direction. You start to feel the inner compass that guides you in the direction of yourself. Until the hand of your inner compass steadily points you in the right direction, you will remain disoriented. You must use the vision of someone, who, by constantly using self-investigation, already achieved a steady position of his inner compass during those difficult periods.

Group work helps us to correct the general picture and motivate us to compile it. Every one of you who comes here and does this difficult work helps us to achieve our goal.

— *I have asked myself, "Would I be able to observe and do this work on my own?" It turned out that I see some fragments, but I cannot connect them on my own. But when I come to group meetings, discuss what I observed during the week, and listen to others, I start to see these fragments better and they connect.*

— Yes, this is so. Group work allows you to manifest and clarify your own picture and the general picture, while a seminar offers you an opportunity to see the results of work completed and mark the direction of future work.

— *I sometimes physically feel the seminar that occurs five hundred miles away from where I am. Something happens to me, and I realize that it is connected to the seminar. I cannot figure out the reasons this is happening to me yet. Later, when someone comes and tells me what happened during the seminar, I start to understand why my body reacted the way it reacted. Seminar happens five hundred miles away, but I experience it here remotely.*

— Even though our groups are in diferent cities, we are one organism. Distance is irrelevant here. The conditioned mind doesn't understand that, but that is the way it is.

— Distance doesn't bother the Soul; it is not bound by any borders.

— People united by the intention of self-investigation form a community. Irrespective of where they happen to be, they constantly interact.

"You acquire experience by talking to us, and you take our money for it. I condemn you for that..."

— Some time ago, you, Alexander Alexandrovich, asked me how I see you. I searched for the answer for a long time, and I finally found it. I'll share my thoughts with you. We have a working group here. We work hard. You come every three months, and not only do you collect what we found, you also take our money. I see that you acquire enormous experience conducting seminars all over the world and communicating with a huge number of different people. You give a lot, but you also receive a lot. That speeds up your development greatly. I, on the other hand, sit here totally constricted, unable to say a word. Moreover, I condemn you for it. Afterwards, I sit by myself thinking, who prevents me from acquiring this experience? I do it myself by condemning you.

— Without me, groups stop working, and people forget everything. I've learned this the hard way.

— I felt it. When you come here, you give us a boost, which we need for future work. Then we disperse and start to work on our own. We get together a week or two later and discuss what we've observed. Later, the group brings all this material to the seminar.

— I want to say something about the money you pay for the seminars. I can apply your model and say to myself, "Why do you charge these fees? You also receive the experience." Yes, I receive, develop, and strengthen it. My experience becomes increasingly valuable. But this doesn't mean you don't need to pay for this experience: I share everything I've gathered with you. And it was not easy to gather all of this and process it. This is priceless experience.

— My thoughts were coming from my poverty stricken part. I can work hard too, but I'd rather spend time on the sofa drinking tea and watching TV. I saw my laziness. Coming to a seminar, I work with my desire. Then I go to work, which I hate. I saw that seminar and work is one for you—it's your life. You receive pleasure from your life.

— I receive both pleasure and displeasure, but I live my life to self-investigate and only self-investigate. This is my main intent, and that's what I push you to do too. When each one of you start to do it, you will finally collect yourself into one whole.

If you don't like your work, I will ask you to look at it like an assignment you need to solve. And the conditions you are in are the best conditions for you to solve it. When you see it and solve it, you will be able to change the givens of your assignment and move on to another assignment.

"Start relating to your daughter the way you wanted your parents to relate to you when you were a little girl..."

— I want to ask Svetlana a question. You have told us that your parents' program was to love boys and not to like girls. You have realized this program in your life: you love your son, and you don't like your daughter. Is that so?

— Yes.

— In reality, you yourself experience your parents' dislike of you, and, being a parent yourself, you experience dislike of your daughter. You carry a familial program of unacceptance of girls and women.

— That's correct.

— Let's go further. On one side, the state of an unloved daughter is very familiar to you. On the other hand, you are also familiar with the state of a mother who doesn't like her daughter very much. You have acquired the experience of not loving from both sides of the duality: mother and daughter. You are in a perfect working condition now. You can connect this duality inside yourself.

114

How can you connect a duality? How can you do it in practice? You can only do it through your heart. You need to feel yourself in her. She is in the same state you are in. You need to come to love your enemy. How can you come to love her? You can only do that by seeing yourself in her. You need to recall this state you were in when you were a child. You need to feel yourself in her. She is you in childhood. She is experiencing what you experienced as a child. You remember this pain and suffering well. She is experiencing this pain and suffering now. You need to fill it. Yes, it is very painful. Yes, you don't want to experience it again. But unless you submerge into this now, you will not be able to get out of it. When you enter this state, ask yourself this question: "How do I see and relate to her now?"

— To start loving her means to love yourself. You can start loving yourself through her. She offers you this opportunity. Whether you will see this as an opportunity or not depends on you.

— *To give love to your daughter is to give love to your inner little girl. That unloved little girl still lives in you.*

— Helen is right. This is of the utmost importance for you now. Your daughter is in the same state you were as a child. If you continue to apply pressure to her, you will oppress your own part. You can start to love yourself through her.

— *I don't understand; how can I start loving her?*

— *That little girl that your mother didn't like is alive in your memory now. This girl gets realized now in the body of your daughter. Don't look at her body. Try to see yourself in her. Start relating to her the way you would want your mother to relate to you. The only way to stop the familial program of not being loved is to do it through yourself.*

— *You wanted your mother to hug and kiss you. You wanted her to talk to you soul to soul. So, do it with your daughter now. Feel it!*

— *I want to emphasize again. Your daughter is you in childhood. You, being forty years old now, are your mother. If your past you is your future you, by connecting them though your current you, you will connect past and future in the present moment. This is what creativity in love and stopping the program of fear*

115

is all about. Start telling her about your life out of a state of love. Feel how she will perceive it. Let her be silent, if need be. Keep telling her about yourself.

— I used to tell her about myself, but I did it on the intellectual level only. I tried to teach and parent her. I reprimanded her for some trivial things. She got bored and quit listening.

— You are in a different state now. You are in the heart. Start to talk to her soul to soul.

— Tell her everything you have. If you feel fear—tell her about it. If you are shaking inside—tell her about it. If you are crying—cry and tell her what you are crying about. Don't hide anything. You will do something new. You will do something your mother didn't do. If you don't do it, you will continue to condemn your mother. Tell her everything the way it is. Tell her what you feel. Explain to her what you feel and what happens inside you. Use simple language. Tell her, "Yes, my position is difficult. I feel my own mother in me who couldn't even hug me." You should tell her everything. You should understand that you are talking to yourself. You should be totally honest with her, i.e. with yourself.

— You have to feel, to talk about it, and to do it. This is a holy trinity.

— My mom taught me and my siblings to relate to my dad like he was some kind of ideal.

Any ideal is an inner district attorney who condemns you to play the role of a slave

— During the socialist era, we were all exposed to and taught communist ideals. There is an ideal, and you need to strive toward it. Someone should be made an ideal role model, and we will strive toward this ideal. The ideal is something unreal, something that doesn't exist. This is how the illusion is created, the illusion people need to strive for and bow to. It is impossible to reach an illusion, as it is unreal. In the end, all your efforts to reach it will boil down to condemnation and guilt. You can always blame and condemn someone, i.e. yourself, for not corresponding to the ideal. An ideal is an unachievable, illusory aim. Running after it, you will always be dissatisfied and condemned. You should be dissatisfied. Otherwise, you will not have anything to strive for. You should always be dissatisfied. You should always have an ideal in front of your eyes, and you should always strive toward it.

— *It is very easy to control someone who strives for a certain ideal.*

— *Everything here is flipped from top to bottom. A man who strives for a certain ideal doesn't see himself. He doesn't understand who he is.*

— People idealize something and pronounce this something, which doesn't exist here, to be very important. Then they say that this something that doesn't exist has to become the subject of your real achievement. How can one achieve something that doesn't exist? But people assume they can achieve it. It's not clear what the ideal is, but you will be constantly blamed for not achieving it. You will always be in the position of a slave. A very common illusion of Christianity is the illusion of "God and God's slave". Socialism in Russia has thrown religion away. It didn't need any competitors. It was religion itself. They have even invented their own trinity: Marx, Engels, and Lenin.

— *Lenin was the first one to be idealized. They took his positive qualities and hid his negative qualities. Those who were doubtful about this ideal were exterminated.*

— The ideal image should be spotless. There should never be a dirty spot on it. People become enslaved by their ideals. Most of us remember how Lenin's ideal was introduced to the Russian population. He was great: handsome and good spirited who loved children. In his youth, he was bright and polite. That's how ideals are created. What kind of duality can we talk about in this case?

— *I don't think he even had those qualities.*

— His image was created as the ideal image for communists or of a saint, if we were to use religious terminology. People should not know anything negative about their ideal. Only few people can know about it, and they will hide it well. The country should only know the ideal image, not the dual personage.

— The circle of those who know anything negative about him is small, and if some information leaks out, they will find out who leaked it.

— They all live in fear: God forbid I'll say something when I am drunk.

— If they find out his tongue was loose, he is going to be striped of power and of every material benefit he had enjoyed. No one wants to experience that. It was a difficult situation. On one side, it is a lie on top of a lie, and on the other side a populace who should have believed in this ideal. There was a huge gap between what was said and what was done.

— People lied to reach certain goals.

— Feelings were turned off completely. Only the intellectual center was working. People used to live in a state of "ought to".

Ideal — an illusory answer to the main question

— What's even more interesting, people believed in those ideals. Moreover, those who created these ideals had to believe in them themselves. The earliest revolutionary believed in their ideals, and as a result the revolutionary "machine" worked. Later, when nonbelievers appeared, the situation changed.

— Not only people believed, they were also scared out of their minds. Many people sincerely cried when Stalin died. Going through the persecutions and hardships of the twentieth century, many of them sincerely believed in Stalin's ideal image. They didn't believe he was responsible for what was going on. The scape goats were found again and again, but his ideal image had to remain spotless.

— The ideal image had to be maintained at all costs. The fall of the ideal image is the fall of the egregor that gave birth to it. When the tsar stepped down from the throne, many White Russian officers lost their footing and committed suicide.

— *They lost the meaning of their existence, and one cannot live without meaning.*

— Our totalitarian society of the proletariat dictatorship was built on communist ideals. The same process occurred in China. While people lived in total poverty almost starving to death, the government of the USSR was building an atomic bomb and sending Sputnik to the moon. Mao's government used fear and manipulation of its people the same way.

This inspiration was built on a certain ideal image in which people believed. As surprising as it seems today, people really believed it. It is very easy to manipulate people using the policy of idealization. The ideal should be embodied physically in someone. People should believe in it. The loss of faith in the ideal leads to destruction of the society built on this ideal. In societies built on the power of one human being, he happens to be the ideal. In so-called democratic societies, a certain symbol plays the role of the ideal. Most frequently nowadays it is the symbol of money.

Japan is another good example. The most honorable death for a soldier is to die for an emperor. The movement of kamikaze started during World War II. This was a new phenomenon for westerners. They couldn't understand it. Japanese were parting with their lives for their ideal. One should strive to achieve one's ideal, and the ultimate goal is to give one's life for it. They thought this was the way to get closer to their ideal. The same logic rules terrorists who blow themselves up in their ideal fight with nonbelievers.

A man needs ideal when he doesn't understand who he really is, i.e. when he doesn't see what really goes on. In this case, he needs a very strong stimulator to understand why he lives. This is the main question of a human being: "Why do I live?" In this case, a certain unachievable ideal gets put forward. This ideal is God. You cannot become God. At most, you can get closer to this ideal. And then, you can justify every action of yours as one that brings you closer to the ideal. That's how terrorists are prepared. So, an ideal is an illusory method that changes the notion of who you really are. Societies that are based on certain ideals are not interested in their citizens understanding who they really are.

— *Everything that does not correspond to the ideals of these societies is destroyed.*

— Societies are built on these ideals. When the ideals go down, societies dissolve. When a proletariat was in power, Lenin was such an ideal. Then Stalin came along. He leaned on the ideal image of Lenin.

— *Fifty years later, we have learned how "ideal" they really were.*

— The mind of a human being who believes in an ideal needs to know only good things about his ideal. As soon as the negative qualities are revealed, a man has two options: to not see these negative qualities, or to dump this ideal and find another one. The consciousness of human beings is idealistic. That's where their fanaticism comes from. Behind it is a state of constant condemnation of surrounding people who cannot compare with their ideal. The presence of an ideal is a great excuse to do what ego loves to do best, i.e. to condemn. While condemning other people, ego tries to get rid of the feeling of guilt. The more guilt it has, the higher the level of condemnation it carries. But this is a vicious cycle: condemnation gives birth to guilt, guilt gives birth to condemnation, etc.

That explains the intricate system of informants widely practiced in the USSR. You have heard about the system of cleansing to which party members were subjected: the cleanliness of the ideal had to be protected. That's exactly what Stalin inspired. This was necessary. Otherwise, people would have noticed that something was off. How was this "something was off" explained? It was explained by the presence of the enemies of the people. They had to be detected and neutralized.

— *A huge mechanism of hatred had been created to take people's mind away from seeing the essence of the situation. It was directed toward seeing the "enemy".*

— The perversity of the notion of ideal itself manifests in an enormous level of condemnation and guilt. People are full of guilt because they feel they cannot compare to the ideal. No one understands that the entire idea is unachievable, but the mind says, "Yes, I am not this, but it is possible to become this." And this enormous guilt has an opposite side—condemnation. Condemnation should be directed somewhere, and we get daily processes conducted by the communist party at every level of society. These processes condemned those who didn't correspond to the ideal image of a soviet citizen. To create an ideal is to create a reason for condemnation and guilt.

— *It is easier to control and manipulate people who feel guilty.*

— This process was conducted on the multiple levels of society. Condemnation and guilt descended all the way to the level of family. Moreover, the level of guilt was so high, that people could not restrain themselves from manifesting its opposite side, i.e. condemnation. The scape goat had to be found and condemned. That's how this mechanism worked.

East and West. How do their ideals interact?

— *What is idealized in the U.S.?*

— Money serves the role of the ideal there. Our ideal used to be "poor, but honest," while in the U.S. money determines everything. The ability to make money is basic there. The duality we are reviewing now is "ideal—material". The idea of the ideal was developed in the USSR. The idea of the material was developing at the same time in the U.S. Those are two sides of one coin, one duality.

When a man is told, "Kill nonbelievers! That will bring you closer to God," he turns into a kamikaze and kills. Try to do that in a democratic society where money is put on a pedestal. It doesn't matter how much money you are going to pay him, he is not going to do it, because who is going to get the money then?

This idealism so strongly developed in Russia gives birth to people who can come up with new ideas, though Americans can realize those ideas better. That's why it is very important for these two opposite sides to interact. One side is full of ideas, while the other can realize these ideas better. One cannot exist without the other.

Look at India with many of its esoteric teachings, and you will see that this is a very poor country. As soon as it starts to move in the direction of business, its idealism will dry up. The number of holy men there is already diminishing; many of them have moved to spiritual business.

The idea of spirituality is still maintained there. Many people go there in search of sacred teachings. Based on this, para-spiritual business structures are getting built.

Interaction of the polar sides of duality leads to a decrease in voltage between them. Activation of duality occurs through the counter position of two of its sides, i.e. each of the sides manifests its polarity vividly. We are entering the time when such an interaction becomes possible. We have an opportunity to see both simultaneously. The work we do now was impossible thirty years ago.

Esoteric consumer society

— We didn't have esoteric, religious, or psychological books. We have this opportunity now. Moreover, Russia was flooded with this literature. The demand was satisfied, and it was satisfied in a very pragmatic way; the literature we see on the market is highly "consumer" driven and oriented. If people want a Siberian-born shaman healer, publishing houses deliver one. Money dictates everything. The desire of the masses should be discovered and satisfied. The market is oriented to satisfy the spiritual desires of most people, and what is consumed by the majority is usually of low quality. We are dealing with the spiritual consumer society.

— *In many cases, people simply accumulate a certain experience. Some of them eventually start to see that something is wrong with this picture: my house is full of esoteric books, but nothing changes in my life—same old, same old.*

— It's not easy to come to what we discuss here because the society itself, whether capitalist or socialist, is a society of consumers. "More goods for people" is the slogan of socialism. "We will satisfy all your needs" is the slogan of capitalism. Both societies are orientated to satisfy consumers' material needs. A human being has needs that come from the old matrix of consciousness. These needs are being satisfied. Moreover, the manufacturers of these needs run after consumers. And I am not talking about material needs alone. Look at the way the recruiters of multiple spiritual sects operate.

— *Olga brought a very good example of a man who surrounded himself with books and believes he knows everything. This man experiences something completely opposite inside. He feels he doesn't know anything. He feels he is walking around in circles. When such a man brings himself to the critical state spreading duality "know—don't know" to the maximum, he can exit. To do that, he needs to refuse the state "I know." The more books a man reads and the more he knows, the more difficult it is to work with him; his mind knows everything or almost everything, and at the same time he doesn't pay any attention to his feelings. He needs to enter the state "I don't know," the opposite polarity of his habitual state of knowledge.*

— *After a certain age, it is almost impossible for a man to say "I don't know." Two sisters who came to our last seminar manifested this well. Both were over fifty-years-old, rich, and of a high social status. One "knew" everything and was eager to express it, while another accepted the state "I don't know." As a result, the first one was unable to take what was going on; she ran away, blaming and condemning everyone and everything, while her sister started to create some amazing things in her life.*

— A man who holds on to and maintains the state of "I know" thinks that he knows who he is. However, when he starts to investigate himself, he suddenly realizes he doesn't possess the true knowledge of who he is. It is extremely difficult to pass this phase. Many of those who stumble at this point live our Process. There is knowledge of abstract character, and they appeal to what Jesus, Buddha, and some other saints have said. They lean on the ideal, i.e. on something that has nothing to do with them. When you shift the topic of conversation and start to discuss who they really are, they run away. As we have discussed already, it is easy to manipulate others by using an ideal. Look, every major religious organization has a huge number of followers.

— *Everything is flipped there. Their attention is turned outside, not inside a human being. "You have to believe in Jesus. Everything else is none of your business." You are just a screw in a big mechanism. Everything has been decided for you already.*

— "You just don't know what Jesus said, and your faith in Jesus is not strong enough." Substitute another name for Jesus in this sentence, and you will understand the mechanism upon which many religious societies are built.

In the presence of multiple political points of view, the main ideal of Soviet society is money and power. Therefore, in the end, everything can be bought and sold. The press clearly demonstrates this.

Materialism and idealism — two sides of one coin

— Let's sort out what people call materialism and idealism here. Materialism represented a lawful religion of the Soviet socialist society. Let's look and see how the philosophy of materialism appeared. It appeared through idealism.

Idealism was necessary for the Russian Revolution to be successful. Trotsky and Bukharin represented idealism. They created the idealistic movement, which excited the masses and directed them toward socialist revolution. When communists took power, Lenin limited the idea of revolution and called every idealist movement opportunistic. Lenin and Stalin afterwards forced many of them out of the country and exterminated those who remained.

As you can see, two opposite sides of this duality are always at war. Each one of them needs something of its own, and to get it, it needs the help of the other side. When the opposite side has done its work, it is not needed anymore and should be eliminated. That happens all the time. The true leader should feel ideal and material as two sides of one coin and support both. A leader's work is to see and maintain the balance between these two sides.

— *Nothing new can happen in our lives while we insist on something being right. When one starts to see the dual nature of a certain duality and to realize its second side, change starts to occur.*

— Every human being represents a factory, if I may use this analogy. There is a side there that is responsible for materialization and a side responsible for the idea. At the same time, we need a director who will accept both sides as two sides of one coin.

— *This is a self-regulating system you teach us to use.*

— Yes. Look at new Russians—they have a lot of money, but they don't have any fresh ideas. They need an idealist who will bring an idea of how and where this money is to be invested. The idealist has a problem of realization. If you look at your own personality, you will see the same war there.

— *War again. Can anything be done here without a war?*

— The old matrix is a matrix of war. The new matrix will ask you to accept both sides as equal sides of one coin.

— *This is the main difference. This is the essence. I understand it now. It took me a while to grasp it. I know it now. I feel it.*

— You can call me a total idealist — I speak of God's Kingdom or a society based on Unconditional Love. What can be more ideal than that?

— *And at the same time, you take money for it.*

— Yes, I combine both sides pretty well. From the point of view of the old matrix, what I discuss here is total idealism. There is something that exists now, and something that doesn't exist yet. I understand that one is impossible without the other. You cannot start something new without leaning on the old. So, we spend most of our time investigating what we have and where we are now, i.e. the old matrix. We investigate it from the point of view of something that doesn't exist yet, i.e. from the point of view of the new matrix of consciousness.

— *I kept telling my husband that he deserved better. When he finally started to achieve better results, he left me for a better woman.*

— Exactly. By telling him that he deserved better, you implied that you were not this "better". He finally found this "better" and left you. You prepared the soil yourself. Everything depends on what we consider as "better". In relationship to the fact that I don't have anything, something is "better", but from the point of view of this "better", "nothing" happens to be "the worst". You should see this interrelationship. Otherwise, you are saying, "Step over me."

— *He quit smoking and he quit drinking. Then he thanked me for showing him the other side of life and he left. He is with another woman now, but his situation is no different from what he experienced with me.*

— In the end, everyone gets back to where he started.

— *I was stuck in this suffering for many years. I could not understand anything.*

— *That's right. Unless your state is changed, you will come back to exactly where you started.*

— I want you to note that we find physical well-being, presence of money, house, cars to be desirable. Later, all of this will flip to the opposite side. This is life in the dual illusion, when people don't see both sides and, in the end, come back to where they started. This is the phase of illusory growth of the ego.

— *I have lost my second husband, and I can see why now. However, the question of why I left my first husband eluded me. I can answer it now. When I was with him, I deserved someone better than him. I can clearly see now that I was mastering the opposite side of this duality at the time. I want to thank you all for helping me to see it.*

— *You can see both sides of this duality now, and you can create something better.*

— You can create something better only when you are aware. The real question is what do you call "better"? By leaning on a duality we don't see, we are just playing, flipping from one polarity to another. Duality plays us.

— *What's good for one man may not be good for another. This is a relative term.*

The average temperature in a hospital is normal

— It is similar to saying that the temperature in a hospital is normal after calculating the average temperature and finding a couple of dead people with a low temperature and five patients with the flu who have a high fever. In the end, the temperature in the hospital is normal. For God it is always good, because for him, as in the hospital, the average temperature is always normal. He balances everything. There is a shortage somewhere and overabundance somewhere else, but the whole system is always in harmony. God is always in equilibrium. The question is where you happen to be.

127

Play anything you want to play and however you want to play it—the average temperature in the hospital is always normal. Everything you do is normal and will be accepted. The diapason of deviation can differ, but the whole system will always remain in a balanced state. You don't need to save the world; everything is okay as it is. People can fight if they want, but God's Kingdom has always existed and will continue to exist. Behind everything is Unconditional Love; it regulates and balances every duality. So, do what you want.

— *It appears that God doesn't have a problem.*

— He created a playground where the life-game can be played, and he observes it. If you want to play war—play it.

— *God loves us the way we are—we are kids playing.*

— Kids pass through different age periods and receive the necessary experience.

— *Observing kids at a kindergarten playground, we see that they play as long as they are interested in the game they are playing. As soon as they lose interest, the game stops. People are interested in the game of war. They are interested in conflict. If most people are interested in this game, it will continue.*

— Nothing will change until the essence of this game and the playground upon which this game is built are clearly seen and people understand what they made out of this playground called "Earth".

— *Once I started to understand and feel this, my life started to change. I started to feel God inside and to create my own playgrounds. Moreover, I started to regulate the games I play on these playgrounds. The key to every game is Unconditional Love and awareness, while the physical body allows us to play these games. This is a super game, and I experience a super state that corresponds to it. I started to live in this game, and my life has changed. This is very interesting. I want to thank you for this experience!*

— That's right. I would ask you to pay special attention to responsibility. People usually view responsibility as a heavy burden, while to **be responsible is to see and understand that you create everything that happens in your life yourself. When you**

understand that, you stop avoiding responsibility; you can do anything you want with a full understanding of how you do it. Until you have this understanding, you will be stuck in one situation or another. The essence of all mechanical games in this reality consists of shifting responsibility to someone else's shoulders while maintaining yourself in a state of condemnation and guilt.

— *The unaware state is a state of no unity and the absence of God.*

— The idea "God left us" is a common idea nowadays. **But it is not God who left us; we forgot Him.** If we were to state it like this, the question appears, "Why did we forget Him?" We can continue to condemn God for leaving us forever, but this will not lead us anywhere. Perhaps, if God left us, we are bad. In that case, another question comes up: "Why are we bad?" All these questions must be sorted out and answered, but few people are willing to do that.

— *Yes, it is much easier to get up, slam the door, and leave.*

— This explains people's desire to create a certain ideal and to ruin it later on. Jesus's story is a good example of this. People made an ideal out of him, and then they crucified him. This can be said about every duality. We can make an ideal out of everything only to destroy it later. This is a favorite pastime in this reality.

The ideal can be made even out of the absence of ideals. That's what so-called nihilists do. In their case, the ideal is in the absence of ideals. One cannot live a mechanical life without an ideal.

You should start seeing things the way they are. This can only be done through awareness. Once you start to become aware, you start to see the interrelationship and interconnection between idealism and materialism.

Money is a means. The main question is "What is it for?"

— *I want to return to the question of money. I need money.*

— I will ask you, "Why do you need money?"

— *Well, I need money to pay for the seminar, for example.*

— Why do you need seminar?

— *I need it to get to know myself.*

— Why do you need to know yourself? What's your true intention? You must have a clear intention. In this case, the intention will create everything necessary. Money is a means to receive something. Everyone wants money, but what is it for? Most people can't answer this question.

There is a common notion here that money is good, and its absence is bad. Everyone wants to have more money. The question of money is not an important question. Money is a means. The main question is "What for?" I say, "Strengthen your intention."

Intention comes from your Soul, while desire comes out of dual personality. Desire leads to anti-desire and activation of duality. Primitive cognition is interested in money, but it is not about the money. It's about what I will get with the money. The next question will be, "Do I really need this?" and "What exactly is it?" But to ask these questions, one must start thinking.

— *My structure associates money with deceit. That's why I don't let it into my life.*

— Honesty is the opposite side of deceit. Money can be honest, but it can also be associated with deceit. You don't want to have money because you base your honesty on its absence—absence of money is a criterion of honesty for you. You think if you don't have money, you are honest. I tell you that there is such thing as honest money, but you cannot comprehend that, because then you would have to move away from the notion that money is always connected with deceit and its absence is a criterion of honesty.

The presence of money does not tell us that a man who has it is dishonest. A very important quality has crystalized in your personality connected to the need to be honest. This is your main card, and you use it quite frequently. There are many different methods to be honest. You invented a method that the presence of money relates to dishonesty, and its absence with honesty. Therefore, you are honest because you don't have money. If you were to acquire money, you would be dishonest. That would destroy your self-identification.

— *I want to point out that your daughter exacerbates your experience. She doesn't have any money, and she easily fools you and other people. She clearly shows you that absence of money is not a criterion of honesty.*

— Duality tightens around your neck like a rope.

— *You cannot understand that there are honest ways to earn money. You emphasize and overplay the honest side.*

— *In looking at the opposite side of this duality—dishonesty, I have to bring your attention to the fact that you ride public transportation for free. If you were to look deeper into it, you would see that you are cheating the bus driver out of his money.*

Criminal police or an honest thief?

— Moreover, you have found a work of "crystal honesty" in the police force. This is your paradox. Dzerzhinsky was a very honest man, and at the same time, the thievery that Russia experienced during his watch was horrendous. The police are supposed to fight for honesty, but we all know what's going on there. Every high-ranking policeman has his own sly methods of working with criminals and receives most of his paycheck from them. The higher the rank, the more money they receive. Previously, the mafia protected "people of value", now this function is carried out by the policemen who receive quite a good paycheck for it. That's where you happen to be now. Now ask yourself who you are: an honest woman or a thief? The question is not about money, because that's what you base your honesty on. See yourself as a thief. The more honest you consider yourself to be, the more a thief you are.

— *I knew that. I felt it. I had to hear that. Thank you.*

— **Personality creates a buffer through which it influences major personal qualities.** Your chief personal feature is "honesty", while a sly way of working with money serves as a buffer for you. Svetlana validates her honesty by using the criterion "money". **You cannot sort out the buffer without addressing the personal feature.** To understand is to see one of the major personal qualities, in this case—honesty. We live in a dual world where major personal qualities are always paired. In your case, we are dealing with the personal quality called honesty. It's polar, opposite side is dishonesty.

— *It looks like I was fooling everyone all lifelong in believing myself to be honest. My daughter brought this to light. I honestly thought I was honest.*

— This is the honesty of one half.

— *It seems to me, I provide myself with life with the help of money; money for me is life. The more money I have, the more I am provided with life.*

— What is life for you? You strengthen personal qualities. A man, who identifies himself with the personality, calls himself what he identifies with, or calls his life what he identifies with. For you, your personality is life. Your life is what you consider yourself to be. We need to look deep into the root cause of this question. The word "life" by itself is meaningless. Otherwise, we are dealing with something abstract; we separate ourselves from life. That's what most people do.

For most people, life means survival

— In reality, for the majority of people, life is survival. People don't talk about life because they don't know what it is; they only know survival. They mistake survival for life. Survival is connected to personality. It is personality that wants to survive, as in essence it is illusory. Money are viewed as means that allow your personage to survive. True life represents an ability to see both sides of the false personality and exiting the borders of what survival requires, i.e. borders of the ego.

— *The question appears, "Why does ego wants to survive?"*

— The one who wants to survive doesn't ask this question; he just survives. Ego structure must preserve its own existence. This is what survival is about. Personality, formed in the mind, fights for one thing only—its own survival. Nothing else interests it. This is the extreme degree of separation.

— *For Sally, the survival of personality, body-mind is connected to the presence of money.*

— Personality is located in the body. Money is required to maintain the life of a body. One must have food, clothing, and shelter. But this is not enough for personality. A human being is a social animal for whom status and the opinions of others, which must be obtained one way or another, are very important. We are currently living in the patriarchal world where money is basic. Therefore, everything and everyone here are oriented toward making money.

— *That's right. It's not only my body that gets me stuck.*

— Status, as an attribute of personality, is easier to obtain through money. It can be obtained by other means, but currently, everything is tied up to money, including status. However, someone can have the status of a good doctor in an undeserved village and be satisfied with it. Svetlana, for example, has a status of an honest woman in the absence of money. That's one way. In Sally's case, status is connected to money, while in Svetlana's case it is connected to their absence.

— *When asked why I gave birth to my second child, I answered, "I did it to survive." My second son allowed me to survive. I needed someone to survive; I started to live for him.*

— To survive only for myself is boring. Therefore, many generic ideas of survival are offered here. Many different states are known on Earth. Mother or father can give up their lives for a child. People may give up their lives for a certain idea. Those are the stages of evolution of human consciousness.

— I mentioned the fact that money is life for me, but my other part wants to die. I feel a desire to die too.

Two opposite directors of one show

— That's the way things are in the reality of a paradox. Someone who sags on one side of a duality, for example, honesty, has another deceitful side that wants to be realized. Every conflict in this world is related to this hidden side, which strives toward its own opening.

— I just understood that this is the side that brings me to your seminars.

— Hitler screamed that Germany will defeat every other country on Earth. At the same time, his shadow side was saying, "Find someone who will defeat you." This side triggered the mechanism of Germany's defeat. We cannot bypass duality. The opposite side will always create excitation and situations to manifest itself.

— I am tired of this fight.

— If you are tired of the fight, you must start seeing the mechanisms of the conflict between your personal parts. The fight will continue until you clearly see all your mechanisms.

— I dont see them. How can I start seeing them?

— Whatever you are afraid of is a manifestation of your opposite side.

— I am afraid of darkness and uncertainty. I have my own house, but I don't live there. I share an apartment with a roommate because I am afraid to be alone.

— What do we do at our readings and meditations when we close our eyes? We submerge into the darkness, i.e. into subconsciousness. We bring everything we have there to the screen of consciousness. You are afraid of the things that you cannot see, i.e. of your subconsciousness. You should look deep inside. You should start to sort things out there.

— In your case, fear is afraid of fear.

— This is fear that produces itself. You should explore it. That's the only way to figure it out. You have a good example near you. Svetlana just passed through two of her strongest fears.

— *I want to thank you. I could have never done it on my own. I was so scared, I had to clench my teeth. But I kept watching …*

— Until you see fear as an illusion, it will continue to control you.

— *Why are we so afraid of the future? Let it be the way it is going to be.*

— Theoretically you are right, but in practice—we are afraid of it. She understands everything intellectually, but she should experience it. Our task in this reality is to acquire a certain experience, i.e. to live through certain situations.

— *You are right. My mind understands everything, but I am afraid to experience it.*

Deceit and honesty

— *I want to share with you what I experienced yesterday. I walked into this experience in full awareness. I entered the duality "honesty—deceit". I felt the impulse coming from my Soul. My mind saw it as total nonsense, but I was outside the borders of the mind. I was observing myself.*

I desperately need money now, and I decided to borrow from someone. I asked myself this question, and the answer came immediately: "Borrow from your neighbor." My neighbor is a gypsy. I spent my whole life with gypsies, and I am afraid of them. The neighbor in question tried to hit on me when we were young, but I was so scared I ran away from him. He lives in a three-story house nowadays. He is very rich. My mom always make fun of me when she sees him, saying that if I were to have married him twenty years ago, I would have been a rich woman by now. That's who I went to borrow money from. Going there, I knew he would fool me. But I went there anyway in full awareness of this fear of being taken advantage of. This fear is very old and persistent. I felt I had to receive this experience. I had to go to him twice. When I came the first time, his bodyguard told me he was out. I came again a couple hours later. I was observing my body.

135

My knees were shaking. My mind was running around saying, "He will never give you the money. You should not have started it." It was funny and scary at the same time. I walked into this situation in full awareness. I was listening to the impulse that was coming from my soul.

When I came after lunch, he was in. We had a long conversation. He did not give me the money, but he offered me a job. Moreover, he said that he always knew I was honest. I could barely contain my laughter when I heard him say I was honest and would never steal from a gypsy. It was an absurd comedy. I have experienced this entire show in detail. First, I was shaking from fear. Then, I was laughing silently. Twenty years ago, I was terribly afraid of this man, but now we were talking amicably. I walked home satisfied. I finally received this experience. I went there in full awareness. I did not get my money. For a whole hour, I dealt with a deception that manifested itself physically through this man.

I had to connect with the duality "deceit—honesty" physically to feel and experience it. I knew from the beginning that he would not lend me the money I needed. I knew he would fool me. But this was a priceless experience. I have accepted this situation with gratitude.

When I got home, I found myself in a state of amazement. My mind did not believe that I went through this old fear of mine and experienced pleasure out of it. Later, I went to the bathhouse and experienced another powerful state. It was late at night. I got into a hot tub and then went outside stark naked. I felt a strong impulse to get on my knees. I did that. I kissed the earth I was kneeling on, and I felt a very strong empathy with it. I saw four elements: earth, wind, water, and fire. I also saw the fifth element in the middle—love. I was one with the Earth. This state is hard to describe in words. I felt it when I was kneeling. I felt I was hugging the entire globe. I experienced love and empathy. I felt the Earth responding to me: we were interacting. I am grateful to everyone here for this experience! Thank you!

— I want to add something. Every one of us experiences earth's gravity. It keeps us here. There is also an opposite state—a zero gravity state. We must learn to feel both states: to feel earth's gravity and to be weightless at the same time. Only by experiencing the gravity free state can we feel how strong the earth

pulls, earth love, i.e. fear is. We can only feel fear—earthly love in weightlessness, when we de-identify with the attraction of the body. We must be in two worlds at once: in the world, but not of this world. I want to thank everyone!

More Books By Alexander Pint

A Mirror for the Personality

Caterpillar to Butterfly: A Way to Yourself

ABC of Self-Investigation

There Are Many of Us, But We Are One

Love - Hate

www.ingramcontent.com/pod-product-compliance
Lightning Source LLC
Chambersburg PA
CBHW070805290326
41931CB00011BA/2137